Anne Robbins

With contributions by
**Allison Goudie, Sarah Herring,
Harriet O'Neill** and **Christopher Riopelle**

Painters'
Paintings
From Freud to Van Dyck

National Gallery Company, London
Distributed by Yale University Press

Contents

Director's Foreword

Artists by definition live with their own pictures, but what motivates them to possess works by other painters, be they contemporaries – friends or rivals – or older masters? Why do some artists collect and what impact does this have on their own work? These are some of the questions that this exhibition sets out to explore. Admiration and influence play their part no doubt, but so too do personal association and kindred-spiritedness, social prestige and the desire to emulate another's achievement. At times the reasons can be more complex or darker and require delving deeply into the artist's psyche where, for example, fierce competitiveness and self-reproach rub uncomfortably against each other.

When Lucian Freud died in 2011 he wanted the National Gallery to receive his painting by Corot, *Italian Woman,* dating from about 1870. Freud had owned works by Degas and Cézanne, as well as by Constable, an artist about whom he knew a great deal, and by his friends, Bacon and Auerbach. The Corot came to the Gallery in 2012 thanks to the generous Acceptance-in-Lieu provision that has enabled many museums and galleries in Britain to acquire remarkable works of art. On its arrival it prompted our curator Anne Robbins to establish how many pictures in the collection had previously belonged to other artists and we were pleasantly surprised to find that about 70 had at some point been in the ownership of painters, some of them very distinguished, from Van Dyck to Matisse, from Reynolds to Leighton. Boucher owned a National Gallery Berchem and Liotard a Van Brekelenkam; Wilkie a Velázquez and Landseer a Giordano. Degas's obsessive desire to possess contributed no less than 14 works by other artists to the National Gallery's collection (and this is apart from seven works by Degas himself, which he had retained until his death in 1917). This is the origin of the exhibition *Painters' Paintings*, and also of the subtitle, which, like the exhibition itself, runs in reverse order, back in time from Freud to Van Dyck.

But in addition to pictures from the Gallery – including Agostino Carracci's enormous cartoon of *A Woman borne off by a Sea God (?)* once owned by Thomas Lawrence, which has not been seen in public for two decades – there are many superb works that have been lent by British and international museums and private collections. We are grateful to all the lenders. I would also like to express our gratitude to The Thompson Family Charitable Trust, Blavatnik Family Foundation, Athene Foundation, Mr Colin Clark, The NDL Foundation, Philippe and Stephanie Camu and The Thornton Foundation, who have made generous contributions to enable the exhibition to take place.

GABRIELE FINALDI

Sir Joshua Reynolds
Self Portrait, about 1780
Oil on panel, 127 × 101.6 cm
Royal Academy of Arts, London
(detail of cat. 50)

Possession:
Painters' Paintings

Anne Robbins

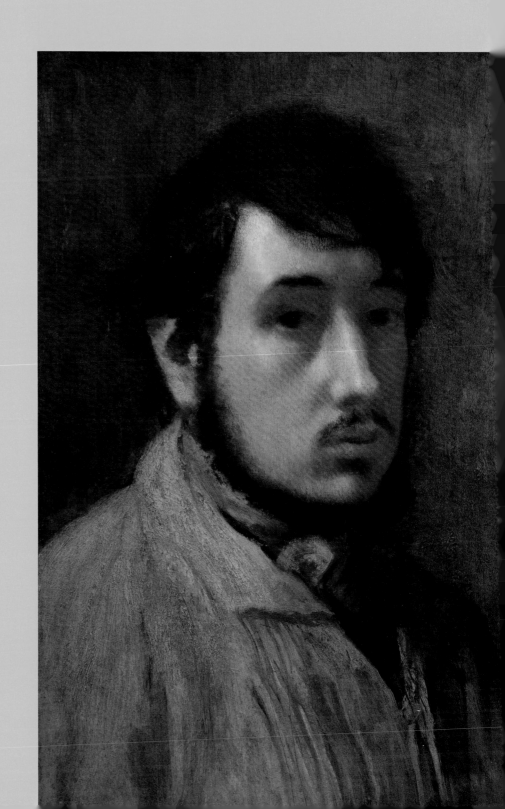

**The possessing [of] portraits by Titian, Vandyke, Rembrandt, & c.,
I considered as the best kind of wealth.**
Sir Joshua Reynolds[1]

Painters have always owned paintings: artists naturally see and are exposed to more art than anyone else, and the pictures collected by painters frequently reflect the development of their own artistic search. This book looks at the artistic impact that ownership makes on painters. What does it mean for a painter to own paintings? And how does the experience of learning from what you own differ from that of seeing works of art in public museums and galleries? The National Gallery, London, was established partially as a resource for artists, and the collections made by painters now form part of its holdings. One such example of a 'painter's painting' is Corot's *Italian Woman* (cat. 2). Owned by Lucian Freud, this work was allocated after his death to the National Gallery, in accordance with his wishes. Since the Gallery acquired it in 2012, the painting's fascinating provenance has attracted considerable attention: it has often been viewed in the light of Freud's own achievements, to the extent that the intrinsic merits of Corot's canvas have almost been eclipsed.

Another much-loved painting in the National Gallery's collection, Edgar Degas's *Combing the Hair* (cat. 12), is striking for its radical use of colour. We know tantalisingly little about the circumstances of Henri Matisse's purchase of the work in the early 1920s, and hardly more about his selling of it some 16 years later. Yet the painting tends to be considered from the vantage point of Matisse's own work, rich in such scenes, not least during his Nice period, when he owned the Degas: women indolently resting in their interiors, rendered in flat areas of colour where red often dominates, that 'piquant colour [...] which hits you in the eye'.[2] The superimposed identity and added layer of interest that are conferred, or imposed, on a painting when it was once in the possession of a painter raise a number of essential issues that demand exploration.

The National Gallery's holdings include more than 70 paintings that fall into this category. Major pictures by nineteenth-century masters that Degas acquired for his own private collection were purchased at the sales in 1918 after his death, and form the core of the Gallery's paintings of this period.[3] Indeed, ever since its foundation in 1824, the Gallery has acquired painters' paintings, often under the guidance of great painters. Some artists, such as Sir Thomas Lawrence, bought pictures for themselves, but also advised influential friends on shaping their own collections, which came to form the nuclei of the National Gallery's holdings. As a result the Gallery's pictures are all, to some extent, painters' paintings: selected by artists (its first directors, from the mid-nineteenth century, were all painters,[4] a function perpetuated to this day by artist-trustees) if not, at some point, owned by painters. Over 80 are discussed in the exhibition, from the collections of eight painters, chosen for their relevance for the artists who acquired them: whether from an emotional, intellectual or spiritual point of view. Looking at these alongside examples of their own work gives us an insight into the inspirations for their art, inviting us to delve deeply into their world.

Fig. 1 | **Hilaire-Germain-Edgar Degas**
Self Portrait, 1857–8
Oil on paper, 47 × 32 cm
The Tia Collection

Gifts and exchanges

Painters frequently receive pictures, as gifts or exchanges from fellow artists,
most often early on in their careers, before such works reach high prices on
the art market. Part of the routine of an artist's life, this trade of pictures obeys
a particular dynamic. These works also tell of their friendships, as attested by
the touching birthday sketch sent by Frank Auerbach to Freud, recording a
moment of camaraderie (fig. 2). Degas's extensive collection contained many
such examples, including Mary Cassatt's *Girl arranging her Hair*, which he
acquired at the 8th Impressionist exhibition in 1886 in exchange for his pastel
Woman bathing in a Shallow Tub.[5]

Portraits were commonly exchanged as a mark of mutual esteem between
painter and sitter. Matisse owned two portraits of himself by André Derain,
dating from their formative years. Famously, Matisse also swapped pictures
with Pablo Picasso, a practice that ceased in 1907, only to be revived several
decades later. In 1941, living in Nice, Matisse sent one of his drawings to Picasso
in Paris, to thank the Spanish artist for looking after his bank vault in the
occupied capital.[6] The following year, Picasso returned the favour when he sent
Matisse his majestic, spectacularly sombre *Portrait of Dora Maar* (cat. 15).

Money was sometimes part of these intricate arrangements between artists. In 1905 Paul Signac set his sights on Matisse's *Luxe, calme et volupté*,[7] a large, classical composition of bathers, which 'would look good on the panelling of [Signac's] dining room'.[8] In exchange, Matisse chose *The Green House, Venice* (cat. 9) and, to make it a fair deal, received 'a banknote of 500 francs' in addition. Likewise, Degas often settled his bills with the dealers supplying him artworks by leaving with them his own paintings and pastels. In 1895 he obtained Eugène Delacroix's imposing portrait of Baron Schwiter (cat. 21) from dealer Montaignac against three pastels with a combined value of 12,000 francs.[9] Edouard Manet's *Woman with a Cat* (cat. 28) and the central fragment of *The Execution of Maximilian* (cat. 30) were both acquired in exchange for Degas's own artworks considered of similar value. In 1789, Sir Joshua Reynolds swapped 'a fancy of his own' for a Giulio Romano from Lord Farnborough, and the same year was paid with a Rubens for his copy of his portrait of *Mrs Siddons as the Tragic Muse*.[10]

Availability and motivations

Assembled randomly at first, thanks to personal ties rather than financial means, painters' collections tend to evolve as their careers develop and their resources increase. They are also shaped by the availability of works. From 1750 onwards, on his return from Italy, Reynolds found himself in a position to embark on serious collecting, but was hindered by the limited supply of pictures in England, as well as paintings for sale abroad. This, and the fact that he often followed his personal taste (sometimes different from his publicly stated opinions), might account for the gaps and chronological leaps in his collection, which did not always follow the academic priorities that he designated in his teachings and writings as President of the Royal Academy of Arts, London.

External factors also had an impact on the formation of the ambitious collection of paintings and drawings that Lawrence was able to amass, such as the remarkable Farnese Gallery cartoons (cat. 45). The French Revolutionary wars and Napoleonic wars flooded the market with pictures from European private collections, from which Lawrence, thanks to his substantial income derived from his successful portrait business, benefited enormously; the paintings he acquired reflect both his large financial means and impressive connoisseurship and taste. Degas's aesthetic preferences and favourite subjects emerge with clarity in the pictures with which he surrounded himself: few Old Masters, although, from the 1890s onwards, he was in a position to afford more of them,[11] but he showed a marked penchant for the work of the great earlier nineteenth-century masters, and for that of his contemporaries. Degas bought paintings by his peers, or by artists younger than himself, in a gesture of support towards his less well-off comrades, assembling a good group of early Impressionist paintings when these were still deemed largely unsaleable. Camille Pissarro, himself the beneficiary of Degas's generosity (cat. 26), later commented: 'Degas [is] so good and so sensitive to others' misfortune [he] has offered to help Paul Gauguin: he bought a painting at his sale'.[12] Other artists, too, rallied to Gauguin's support, notably the Nabis painters Maurice Denis, Paul Sérusier, Pierre Bonnard, Ker-Xavier Roussel and Edouard Vuillard, who in 1891 all contributed to the joint purchase of Gauguin's *Landscape with Two Breton Women* of 1889.[13] However, their plan to share it by having it in their respective homes on a rota basis proved unpractical; in 1905, having probably drawn lots to establish who would have sole ownership, Vuillard purchased the shares of the other four to become the picture's only owner.

Collecting as homage

Reflecting companionships and attachments as well as chance meetings, painters' paintings often pay homage to former masters: personal mementos much valued as moving tributes to figures of inspiration. Matisse acquired several paintings by Pierre-Auguste Renoir, whose acquaintance he had made on his arrival in Nice in late 1917, and to whose house he was a regular visitor.[14] Four self portraits by Reynolds, owned by his one-time pupil Lawrence, attest to the same loyalty towards a former master and mentor. Lawrence's association with Reynolds and his collection – as well as those of early patrons and clients who let him have access to their riches – might have instilled in him a longing to collect himself. In the same way, Sir Anthony van Dyck, having encountered the work of Titian in Peter Paul Rubens's house, followed the latter's example and went on to gather his own 'Cabinet de Titien' (cats 61 and 62).[15] The inventory drawn up shortly after Van Dyck's death lists 19 works by Titian, mostly portraiture – 'fifteen or sixteen choice portraits by Titian' – mythologies and religious pictures, including *Perseus and Andromeda,*[16] an Ecce Homo and some landscapes in watercolour.[17] In addition, Van Dyck copied four works by Titian, a characteristic way for artist-collectors to appropriate works of art they coveted but could not obtain. Aiming for exhaustiveness in the picture gallery he was creating for himself, Rubens had painted replicas of Titian's portraits because he did not own any.[18] This solution was thought more suitable than compromising on the quality of the pictures they pursued, or resorting to the acquisition of minor painters and paintings.

Degas's collection provides another example of the closely intertwined acts of copying and owning pictures. The 1890s saw Degas, now able to rapidly acquire major paintings by nineteenth-century masters, looking out for autographed copies or artists' repetitions of pivotal works he himself had copied decades earlier as a student, such as Jean-Auguste-Dominique Ingres's *Angelica saved by Ruggiero* (cat. 18).[19]

Degas's assortment of pictures was both wide in scope – encompassing El Greco and Ingres as well as radical, idiosyncratic artists such as Paul Cézanne (cat. 33) and Gauguin (cat. 32) – and tightly focused, with groups of works by Delacroix and Manet covering their whole oeuvre. However, the collection was uniform in terms of media: works on paper and sculptures (the inventory drawn up after his death lists bronzes by Antoine-Louis Barye[20]). In contrast, the paintings with which Matisse surrounded himself were part of a collection that comprised objects originating from different epochs and cultures. With his all-encompassing gaze, Matisse treated pictures as he did textiles or African artefacts; his visual discernment transcended high and low art, ignoring any hierarchy other than that of aesthetic quality.[21]

The desire to possess

Matisse's taste evolved constantly; he bought and sold from dealers, parting with once-cherished pictures in order to acquire more, or for profit. His sale of Gauguin's *Young Man with a Flower behind his Ear* (cat. 8) – which he had had in mind to swap for a Renoir as early as 1908[22] – allowed him to make further purchases after 1915 (cat. 12). Reynolds, similarly eager to improve his holdings, frequently sold pictures from his private collection to buy better ones. 'I considered myself as playing a great game', he recalled, 'and, instead of beginning to save money, I laid it out faster than I got it, in purchasing the best examples of art that could be procured ...'[23] He did, however, occasionally make a profit from speculating on pictures, with which he supplemented his income. Lawrence also felt the thrill of the auction house, bidding relentlessly, driven by his sheer desire for acquiring pictures.[24] He was often in debt on account of his overarching collecting aspirations.[25] Van Dyck displayed the same voraciousness, revealing in a letter of 16 April 1631 his 'urgent' need to know whether a Titian portrait he was coveting might be available.[26] Many accounts by friends and witnesses attest to Degas's compulsive buying habits, which increased as he advanced in age and was progressively losing his eyesight, keeping him away from the studio. 'Fired up'[27], Degas went to the greatest lengths to acquire the paintings he desired: 'Degas carries on ... buying, buying; in the evening he asks himself how he will pay for what he has bought that day, and the next morning he starts again'.[28] This tenacity allowed him to gather four fragments of Manet's *Execution of Maximilian* (cat. 30), which had been cut and dispersed after the artist's death, and to reassemble them. 'You are going to sell me this,' Degas ordered the dealer Ambroise Vollard, determined to buy from him the central fragment as well as the legs of the sergeant, which were some of the missing pieces in the puzzle he was set on piecing together.[29] When Ingres's superb portraits of Monsieur and Madame Leblanc came up for auction,[30] Degas entered a gentleman's agreement with his friend, the sculptor Albert Bartholomé, by which they would each buy one portrait of the pair; it was agreed that 'each would have his own picture. But Bartholomé never dared to insist on the point with Degas, who jealously kept both Mr and Mrs'.[31] His acquisitiveness bordered on addiction, as he threatened his dealer Durand-Ruel: 'Do not deprive me of the little copy after Ingres. I really need to have it',[32] or announced in a tone of frenzied triumph:

> Here is my new Van Gogh, and my Cézanne; I buy! I buy! I can't stop myself. The trouble is that people are beginning to know about it and are bidding against me: they know that when I want something, I absolutely must have it.[33]

The critic Arsène Alexandre, himself a collector and visitor to Degas's house, described him as 'possessed by the devil of collecting, rarer than one would think among artists'.[34]

Nevertheless, the history of art is sprinkled with not-so-rare stories of struggling artists resorting to extreme measures to buy art; for instance, the sculptor Jacques Lipchitz, in dire financial straits, gave up four meals in order to purchase not a painting, but a much-desired African mask in Paris in 1912.[35] Matisse had to make similar sacrifices to acquire the art he 'needed',[36] going as far as to pawn his wife's ring – his wedding present to her – to pay for Gauguin's *Young Man with a Flower behind his Ear* (cat. 8) from Vollard in 1900, having already used her dowry to buy the all-important *Three Bathers* by Cézanne (cat. 7) the previous year.[37] Matisse denied this version of the story, later told by Gertrude Stein.[38] Yet his urge to possess these pictures and the prospect of enjoying them at leisure led him to hunt them doggedly. From the very moment he saw the Cézanne in Vollard's gallery, it eclipsed Vincent van Gogh's *Les Alyscamps* that he had envisaged buying.[39] Matisse went away without purchasing the Cézanne, only to return to Vollard a few weeks later, ready to make the deal.[40] It took him six months to settle the payment: 'You're off your head, old boy, take that back to Vollard', his friends advised, 'and if he buys [it] back at the purchase price, you'll be in luck'. Matisse replied: 'Either I'm wrong, or I knew what to choose.'[41] Gripped by its uncompromising modernity, Matisse treasured his Cézanne,[42] keeping it close by as he developed his own artistic style.

Fig. 3 | Sébastien Bourdon
The Return of the Ark, 1659
Oil on canvas, 105.3 × 134.6 cm
The National Gallery, London

Teaching tools

Painters' paintings not only inspired colleagues, but also students, for whom they were a prime resource for learning. Cézanne's *Three Bathers* nourished Matisse's reflections on art, and helped him formulate the artistic theories that were to guide his career and underpin his teaching in the academy that he had founded in 1907. 'What interests me', Matisse wrote in 1908, 'is neither still life, nor landscape, but the figure',[43] extolling the 'order and clarity' in Cézanne's pictures.[44] During this brief spell – the Matisse Academy was short-lived – Matisse based his teaching on 'Cézanne's architecture, masonic plasticity, his unique vision and unexcelled meticulous execution'.[45] One of his students, Max Weber, remembered how, on rare occasions, an emotional Matisse would invite pupils to his own studio, to show them 'with modesty and deep inner pride' the pictures he owned. *Three Bathers* constituted the climax of the visit:

'his [Matisse's] silence before it was more evocative and eloquent than words. A spirit of elation and awe pervaded the studio at such times'.[46]

Between 1769 and 1790, Joshua Reynolds had included in the *Discourses* he gave to the students of the Royal Academy, in his role as President, discussion about some of the pictures in his collection. 'In my opinion', he declared, 'there is not one picture in this collection which does not possess some part of the art that is worth the attention of the Students in Painting, it is upon this principle they were collected ...'.[47] In 1788 Reynolds described Sébastien Bourdon's *Return of the Ark* (fig. 3) as a work 'in which the poetical style of landscape may be seen happily executed',[48] and in his eighth *Discourse* referred to 'a picture which I have of Rubens',[49] that is, *Landscape by Moonlight*, which he had acquired a few months earlier and rated highly.[50] It seems the paintings commented on by Reynolds were actually brought to his audience, since he refers to 'making observations [...] on the pictures now before us'.[51] In the *Discourses*, Reynolds's Old Master paintings provided the foundation for the theory of art that he was presenting, in which, among other principles, he distinguished between the curious and the admirable[52] – based on the career of Raphael[53] – and differentiated between what he described as the 'ornamental' and the 'great Style'.[54] He was thus organising his paintings intellectually as well as physically, ordering them according to academic priorities he had defined – in which history painting dominated, mirroring the large preponderance of such pictures in his collection[55] – and using them to teach his students about the hierarchy of art historical genres.

Legacy

Keen to establish their credentials as connoisseurs, some artists also sought to align themselves with those whose work was in their possession. While prompting them to engage with art history, these paintings invited them to question their own place in it, a process that often led to an affirmation of position in a noble lineage of great artists to which they saw themselves as heirs or disciples. Lord Leighton, by hanging his unfinished yet spectacular portrait by Reynolds of Rockingham and Burke in his staircase hall, was alluding to his predecessor, first President of the Royal Academy, and in so doing proclaimed himself as heir to Reynolds's artistic legacy.[56]

The subsequent fate of these lovingly, tirelessly assembled collections was naturally always of prime importance for the artists. Reynolds, who confided in old age that his collection 'had been the business of [his] life',[57] had envisaged it as a permanent resource for his students; its future preoccupied him greatly as he advanced in years. As James Northcote wrote:

> So anxious was Sir Joshua Reynolds for the diffusion of a good taste in art and that future students might find a practical commentary on those precepts which he had now ceased to deliver, that he, in the most liberal manner, offered to the Academy this collection at a very low price, on the condition that they would purchase the Lyceum in the Strand for the purpose of constructing an exhibition room.[58]

The latter was never built, the offer was declined and the collection dispersed in several sales after the artist's death.[59] George Frederic Watts, who owned pictures by Old Masters and by his contemporaries, was more concerned about the works being enjoyed by a wider public than keeping them to himself. In 1861, he presented to the National Gallery *A Knight of S. Stefano* (cat. 41),

Fig. 4 | **French (?)**
Profile Portrait of a Young Man,
possibly about 1580
Oil on paper mounted on canvas,
38.5 × 28.5 cm
The National Gallery, London

then attributed to Pontormo, having 'owned it for some time'.[60] Twenty years later he donated a second painting, a portrait then believed to be by François Clouet (fig. 4), in another act of disinterested philanthropy from an artist whose pictures were 'his only fortune', yet who was determined to leave them to the nation.[61]

The sales after Degas's death revealed the extent to which he had amassed paintings, both in terms of quantity and quality; these works were sold in Paris in 1918 in three important auctions, as the First World War was still raging. As early as the mid-1890s, concerned with the long-term future of his collection, Degas had considered founding a museum, but this scheme never came to fruition. While anxious to perpetuate his collection beyond his death, the artist was nonetheless reluctant to make his beloved pictures too widely accessible, favouring a venue far from Paris and its crowds.[62] The opening in 1903 of a museum dedicated to the work of his friend Gustave Moreau, a stone's throw from Degas's house and dismissed by him as a mausoleum, dissuaded Degas from pursuing his plan.

Painters' paintings at home

In November 1897 Degas had moved to new, vast lodgings on the rue Victor Massé,[63] where he had already had a studio for the last seven years; the house was arranged in three apartments over three floors, as his friend Walter Sickert explained: 'one to live in, the one above for his collection, and, at the top of the building, his studio.' Degas's most treasured pictures were thus kept separate from his own works, in a distinct space. Sickert went on to describe this shrine, in which he had 'sometimes [...] threaded [his] way' with Degas, 'by the light of a candle, through the forest of easels standing so close to each other that [they] could hardly pass between them, each one groaning under a life-sized portrait by Ingres, or holding early Corots ...'[64] The highlights of the collection were placed in a semicircle, with more paintings hung on the walls.[65] In this extraordinary private museum, always locked, 'closed, defended, shut away',[66] Degas venerated his pictures at leisure, attentive, beyond the apparent chaos, to their good maintenance and protection.[67] He arranged for his pictures to be restored by trusted conservators, to ensure their good physical preservation.[68] His loving care and dedication are also manifest in the way in which, in the 1890s, much like a curator, he recorded and documented his collection, making practical notes, keeping sales catalogues and all documentary material relating to it.[69]

The setting of the first-floor gallery in Degas's home did not mean that pictures were excluded from his living quarters; photographs show paintings hanging in his drawing room too.[70] Witnesses described how pictures were displayed in his bedroom, including the small portrait of Francis Poictevin by Jacques-Emile Blanche (cat. 31), and Corot's *Roman Campagna* (cat. 25): these may have been the works with which he felt the closest, most emotional connection. Likewise, Lucian Freud could see Corot's *Italian Woman* (cat. 2) from his bed, along with the small bronze portrait by Degas (fig. 5) which he bought in 1995; this proximity to the most intimate space of the house probably demonstrating the highest, most personal level of admiration.

Not all painters felt the same. In contrast, Lord Leighton chose to adorn his bedroom with inexpensive reproductions of pictures, reserving the most public areas of his house for the paintings he had acquired. He purchased Corot's *Four Times of Day* (cat. 36) while the construction of his house was underway, and the four pictures may have formed part of the architectural scheme for the ground-floor drawing room for which they were intended;[71] they were originally painted for the dining room of the artist Alexandre Decamps, Corot's friend, at his house at Fontainebleau. On Leighton's walls the panels formed a single entity with their surroundings, also serving to bolster Leighton's reputation as a refined, enlightened gentleman. Thus, the sophisticated setting emphasised the brilliance of the pictures on display, as well as Leighton's personal genius. The drawing room, with its concentration of French pictures, hinted at his cosmopolitan background and years of training on the Continent. Rather than hoarding his masterpieces, Leighton flaunted them, making them widely accessible in his newly built house, which was specially conceived for their display. Placed conveniently adjacent to the studio where he would receive his wealthy clients, the picture gallery on the first floor was the showcase for his Old Masters (cat. 39).

Commercial strategies and tactics of self-promotion were also at play in Reynolds's home, a fashionable town house at 47 Leicester Square, London, where he lived for the last 30 years of his life.[72] There, contemporary works such as Thomas Gainsborough's *Girl with Pigs* (cat. 59) were displayed in a cabinet of Old Master pictures, stressing the links between such English genre scenes and the sentimental simplicity of Bartolomé Esteban Murillo's art.[73] Reynolds's pictures played an essential role in promoting himself as a gentleman-connoisseur and also served his business interests. When working on a portrait, some of his Old Master paintings would hang nearby, carefully chosen to prompt conversation with his client. Reynolds would probably go as far as to select the picture on display to match the taste of his sitter. This was a successful commercial strategy: the painter would bill his clients not just for their portraits, but also for the Old Master works he occasionally sold to them at the same time.[74]

Fig. 5 | **Hilaire-Germain-Edgar Degas**
Portrait of a Woman: Head resting on One Hand, cast after 1918
Bronze, 12.3 × 17.5 × 16.2 cm
Leeds Museums and Art Galleries (Leeds Art Gallery)

Despite the limited amount of information and contemporary material about how earlier artists lived with the pictures they owned, enough is known to establish that they paid great attention to their display and arrangement at home. Van Dyck gathered his Titians in one room, acknowledging his reverence for the Venetian master in this 'Hall of Honour'.[75] When he moved to London in 1635, his 'Cabinet de Titien' followed suit, and was transported to and reinstalled at his house in Blackfriars.[76] Lawrence turned the attic of his house into a large studio in which Old Master paintings did not seem to feature. But, in the rest of his home, he lived among the pictures and full-scale casts of antique sculptures he collected.

The distinction between house and studio was rather more fluid in Matisse's successive homes. Photographs taken in Nice show the artist working at his easel, with some of the paintings he had acquired on the walls, in groupings that kept changing, reflecting the evolution of his collection. This, and his frequent moves from one house or apartment to another, might justify the informal, un-museum-like arrangement of the pictures. They were displayed casually (a photograph[77] of Matisse's home at Place Charles Félix in Nice shows Cézanne's *Three Bathers* (cat. 7) double-hung with Renoir's *Portrait of Suzanne Valadon*,[78] both unframed), yet not haphazardly: Matisse hung his pictures with a full awareness of their formal relationships, next to fragments of textiles and exotic artefacts.

Owning a painting, rather than enjoying it momentarily, meant that these painters had the freedom to display, but also displace, them at leisure. Reynolds brought his Old Master pictures when delivering his *Discourses* at the Royal Academy; Matisse, too, carried around the pictures he owned, taking them to the elderly Renoir in 1918: 'Renoir's head with the corset; [...] he was happy to see it so well preserved'.[79] He would ask Renoir for his opinion, and together they would judge their merits, prompting, no doubt, fascinating conversations on the artists Matisse revered so much as to own their pictures. Matisse wrote to his wife how, upon being brought Cézanne's *Three Bathers*, Renoir declared it 'very beautiful, highly worked, splendid landscape [...] I looked like a nabob showing his treasures. Well. I packed it all away and said goodbye'.[80]

Emulation or rivalry?

The luxury of repeated viewing, of unhurried contemplation and contact with the pictures artists owned, opened up infinite and essential possibilities of engaging and learning from these works. The paintings and drawings that Reynolds had gathered formed an inexhaustible source not just for teaching, but also for his own study purposes, providing him with a stock of motifs, themes and compositions from which to borrow.[81] The numerous studies for Ingres's *Apotheosis of Homer* (cats 19 and 20), assembled by Degas, supplied him with a repertory of poses. From these partial studies Degas may have drawn the idea for his own fragmented compositions, remarkable for the asymmetrical, daring cropping of figures. The nudes and portraits Degas collected are echoed in his own artistic production, where these genres dominate (figs 1 and 6).

Looking at and learning from the works in his possession, Lawrence developed his stunning, assured brushwork, a loose, fluid impasto reminiscent of Rubens and Van Dyck, distinctively 'old-masterly', with a rich palette and broad brushstrokes (fig. 7 and cat. 49).[82] Degas acquired not only a number of Delacroix's greatest masterpieces, but also some of the artist's actual palettes, to better understand his working methods and prodigious combinations of colours. Beyond their function as ornaments of taste and symbols of social rank,

Fig. 6 | Hilaire-Germain-Edgar Degas
Portrait of Elena Carafa, about 1875
Oil on canvas, 70.1 × 55 cm
The National Gallery, London

the paintings in Leighton's and Reynolds's possession helped them comprehend how pictures were made. Leighton, who had met Corot in Paris, never forgot his recommendation to use a specific pigment, 'laque de gaude', a transparent yellow that allowed subtle effects of translucency in his skies.[83] His unhindered access to Corot's *Four Times of Day* (cat. 36) and to his small *Evening on the Lake* (fig. 8) enabled him to explore the French artist's technique at first hand. Reynolds, too, engaged with his Old Master paintings on the most material level. Curious to decipher his predecessors' technical secrets and painterly effects, he attempted to emulate them in his own pictures. To do so, he needed to experiment, thus 'investigating' his Old Master paintings by rubbing elements of them to find out how they were made.[84] As James Northcote stated, 'each painting thus investigated was, of course, totally destroyed'.[85] With little deference for the integrity of the original work, Reynolds would rework a painting while attempting to restore it, enhancing it – or so he hoped – while learning about its technique in the process. Bourdon's *Return of the Ark* (fig. 3) and Van Dyck's *Horses of Achilles* (cat. 57) show the evidence of passages attributable to Reynolds himself.[86] By physically 'improving' these paintings, Reynolds was challenging their creator's original intentions – uncovering the technical mysteries of the masters, but also imposing his own ideas and style.

Fig. 7 | **Sir Thomas Lawrence**
John Julius Angerstein,
aged over 80, 1824
Oil on canvas, 91.5 × 71 cm
The National Gallery, London

'Works of art', Reynolds said, 'are models you are to imitate and at the same time rivals you are to combat'.[87] Matisse and Picasso would not have denied this statement. When they first swapped works, both artists felt much concerned about, if not threatened by, each other's genius. The *Portrait of Marguerite*[88] that Picasso had swapped with Matisse in 1907 hung in his studio, where the Spanish artist and his friends would 'attack' it with sucker darts from a toy pistol – 'Pop! Straight into Marguerite's eye', recalled a companion – in a seemingly playful, but actually very serious competition.[89] Degas's dialogue with the paintings he owned could also turn into a duel, in which jealousy could prompt him to return pictures he had acquired from his contemporaries if upset or offended (cat. 31).[90]

Stimulation and inspiration

Paintings owned by painters come to embody not just their creator, but their subsequent artistic possessors. What we own reveals who we are and, for painters, sheds light on how, what and why they paint. Freud's own pictures are a striking demonstration of how close paint can come to flesh, how vividly

18 | PAINTERS' PAINTINGS

one can evoke the other, re-creating life itself under a painter's brush. We know how, at the end of his life, virtually blind, Degas would touch the pictures he owned, identifying them by feeling their texture and surface, following their contours.[91] In the same way, Freud needed the physical presence not just of sitters, but also of pictures, which he apprehended in their full materiality. Impressed by John Constable's 'awareness' of paint[92] – the 'vital element without which painting can't exist; PAINT'[93] – Freud felt the emotional weight of possessing a tangible object by a master painter, its visceral quality and overwhelming presence. Owning a painting, for a painter, engenders the deepest possible level of engagement with it, in what can be an intimate and intensely creative dialogue.

The uniqueness of a painter's collection of paintings, as opposed to one assembled by a collector-connoisseur, lies in the relationship between the pictures they collect and their own artistic production. Reynolds and Lawrence were great connoisseurs;[94] the pictures in their collections reflect, to an extent, the time and context in which both artists lived. Yet their approach was more than just scholarly; it was influenced by their own artistic discrimination, exceeding the parameters of the usual tastes of the period. Leighton was one of the earliest collectors of Corot in Britain, and the pictures he gathered stand outside the confines of conventional collecting in the Victorian age.[95] Freud turned his attention to Constable's portraits (cat. 5), a lesser-known aspect of the celebrated landscapist's work. It is sometimes argued that in Lawrence the instincts of the artist and the scholar were in conflict with each other, impeding his creative work, whereas in Van Dyck (fig. 9), Reynolds or Degas they worked in harmony, stimulating their artistic production. Reynolds borrowed from 'his' Rembrandts their profound contrasts, deep shadows and sharp croppings (cat. 50), while Degas achieved an accomplished synthesis of the lessons he learned from 'his' works by Ingres and Delacroix: smooth lines, calculated yet dynamic compositions and expressive colours. Leighton demonstrated his complete absorption of Corot's art in the style, elegant construction and crisp, precise touch of his landscape studies (cats 37 and 38).

In an astonishingly creative dynamic, the pictures painters owned assisted their search for new forms. Cézanne's *Three Bathers* (cat. 7) helped Matisse

Fig. 8 | **Jean-Baptiste-Camille Corot**
Evening on the Lake, about 1872
Oil on canvas, 25.1 × 36.2 cm
The National Gallery, London

to conquer unexplored artistic territories. Its long-lasting impact on Matisse's whole oeuvre, painted as well as sculpted, proved groundbreaking:

> If only you knew the moral strength, the encouragement that his [Cézanne's] remarkable example gave me all my life! In moments of doubt, when I was still searching for myself, frightened sometimes by my discoveries, I thought: 'If Cézanne is right, I am right'; because I knew that Cézanne made no mistake.[96]

Fig. 9 | **Sir Anthony van Dyck**
Lord John Stuart and his Brother,
Lord Bernard Stuart, about 1638
Oil on canvas, 237.5 × 146.1 cm
The National Gallery, London

Throughout his career Matisse sought to acquire pictures that confirmed the direction in which his art was moving. In the 1920s for instance, when his work took a more naturalistic turn, so did his collection.[97] Decades later, in 1949, while working on the décor of the chapel in Vence, in south-east France, Picasso's portrait of Dora Maar (cat. 15, which Matisse had received from the artist a few years earlier) hung close by. Picasso's painting, notable for 'the anguish of the figure, the terrible expression of [the] face'[98] – qualities we do not typically associate with Matisse – assisted Matisse to achieve the pathos with which he wanted to imbue his work on the chapel's Stations of the Cross.

In the same way, Freud sought the qualities that marked his own production in the work of the artists he admired, and whose art he acquired. We can characterise these as an apparent awkwardness, as well as a concrete sign of a long, painstaking elaboration of the painting, the slow maturation of a composition.[99] These qualities are evident in Cézanne's *Afternoon in Naples* (cat. 3), a painting that verified and supported Freud's own artistic methods and achievements, and became a vital stamp of approval on his own creative work. Cézanne's brothel scene was the trigger for one of Freud's most ambitious compositions, *After Cézanne* (fig. 10), started within weeks of Freud buying the picture at auction in 1999.[100] In it, the painter explicitly confronts Cézanne's small, enigmatic painting, expanding on a trend he began in the 1980s with his *Large Interior, W11*,[101] and followed by more such 'paraphrases' after the masters, as he called them. These pictures saw Freud distance himself from sheer autobiography to explore dramatic tension in figural compositions, in situations not of his own invention but borrowed from great artists of the past. The next step of this approach entailed basing his own pictures on works of art he actually owned. A 'cousin', as Freud described it, 'related but very different',[102] *After Cézanne* re-adapts Cézanne's composition on a vast scale, re-creating what Freud called 'the illusion of simplicity' in a clearly staged, re-enacted play.[103] Enlarging the picture with an extra piece of canvas, Freud here questions the process of representation itself, in a complex *mise en abîme* where the painting's clumsy format echoes the ungainliness of Cézanne's picture.

Looking at an artist's collection can be compared to entering a mind, and accessing a usually overlooked dimension of his or her activities, yet it is one of the most essential as it offers critical clues for a correct, deep and multifaceted understanding of their art. Painters' paintings represent the very continuation of their artistic production; ultimately and most fruitfully, they constitute works of art in themselves, where the genius of an artist has assembled the products of other artists and, as a result, has been able to bring to life a different work altogether. Painters' paintings form ephemeral groups of artworks, chosen – thus, created – with artistic skill, sensitivity and inventiveness on the part of the painter who selected them. They represent the most secret kind of self portrait: objects that do not bear the mark of the artist's own hand, yet convey the presence of their owner with the most intriguing material truth. Corot's *Italian Woman* (cat. 2) unmistakeably conjures up Freud, reflecting his very self and exposing Freud with astonishing honesty.

Fig. 10 | Lucian Freud
After Cézanne, 1999–2000
Oil on canvas, 214 × 215 cm (irregular)
National Gallery of Australia, Canberrra

Lucian Freud

1 | **Lucian Freud**
Self Portrait: Reflection, 2002
Oil on canvas, 66 × 50.8 cm
Private collection

With its complex levels of representation and layered paint surface, *Self Portrait: Reflection* counts among Freud's (1922–2011) most arresting images of himself. It is also a timeless meditation on the artist's identity as a painter, demonstrating the impact of the great Western tradition of painting on his own work. This tradition was represented in Freud's home with pictures from across the centuries that testified to his artistic affinities: works by his contemporaries Bacon and Auerbach, a small boudoir scene by Cézanne (cat. 3) and Corot's robust *Italian Woman* (opposite).

Their visceral quality is echoed in Freud's uncompromisingly honest self portrait: febrile, intense and striking for its compressed nervous energy and remarkably dense texture. The rough, grainy medium almost engulfs the sitter; the background's superbly rugged, geological surface replicates the dense crust of paint that had built up over the years on the walls of Freud's studio, where he used to wipe his palette knife. This is a reflection on life itself, on the material presence of paint and on the passing of time. AR

2 | **Jean-Baptiste-Camille Corot**
Italian Woman, or *Woman with Yellow Sleeve (L'Italienne)*,
about 1870
Oil on canvas, 73 × 59 cm
The National Gallery, London

Corot, who is best known today for his landscapes, was also an accomplished painter of figures. This Italian woman, probably a professional model dressed in traditional costume, fills the entire canvas with her formidable presence. The painting's pronounced volumes and abrupt, rough-hewn brushwork impressed Freud, who bought it at auction in 2001. 'A portrait isn't just a flat image,' he declared a few years later. 'It is a person. It needs to have dimension.'

As if carved out from a dark background, this hieratic, inscrutable *Italian Woman* commands attention. The picture presided over Freud's drawing room on the top floor of his house, where it held its own against paintings by Auerbach and sculptures by Degas.

For Freud, this painting was charged with great emotional value. He left it to the British nation in gratitude for giving his Jewish family a refuge from persecution in 1933. AR

3 | **Paul Cézanne**
Afternoon in Naples
(*L'aprés-midi à Naples*), 1876–7
Oil on canvas, 29.5 × 39.5 cm
Private collection

Freud acquired this small, little-known painting by Cézanne in 1999, attracted by its lively handling of paint as well as by its provocative subject matter, which he thought 'erotic and funny'. In what looks like a brothel, two lovers rest entwined, while a maid enters the room bearing a tray. As indicated by the awkward, theatrical poses and staged composition, framed by curtains, this erotic fantasy echoes the 'morose Eros' – as one journalist wrote – of Freud's own nudes on dishevelled sheets. Captivated by his Cézanne,

Freud soon started working on an ambitious painting based directly on it, *After Cézanne* (fig. 10), which re-creates and reinterprets the scene: a 'paraphrase' imbued with the same enigmatic, cynical humour, yet intensifying the tension between the protagonists. For a time Freud pinned a reproduction of his Cézanne to the encrusted walls of his studio, where it almost disappeared into the thick layers of paint; the canvas itself hung in his drawing room. AR

4 | **Lucian Freud**
After Breakfast, 2001
Oil on canvas, 41 × 58.4 cm
Private collection

In his so-called 'naked portraits', which he believed revealed the character of his sitters more fully, Freud fused two art historical genres well familiar to him. Here, observed from above, the model lies naked on crumpled sheets. As if sheltering from the threatening, arrow-like verticals of the floorboards, her legs are folded, approaching a foetal position. Her attitude recalls the female courtesan's pose in Cézanne's *Afternoon in Naples* (opposite), which Freud then owned, while the strict diagonals of the armchair allude to the upturned wooden chair in the Cézanne. Likewise, both paintings record a particular moment of the day.

It is undoubtedly the painting's startling realism and tactile quality that liken it most to the great nineteenth-century masters of the genre, including Courbet, whose 'shamelessness' Freud admired. Freud breathed life into his nude and gave it consistency by using a granular medium, Cremnitz White, which he favoured. The fabulously raw, gritty surface contrasts with the restrained and delicately balanced palette. AR

5 | **John Constable**
Portrait of Laura Moubray, 1808
Oil on canvas, 44.5 × 35.5 cm
Scottish National Gallery, Edinburgh
Accepted by HM Government
in lieu of Inheritance Tax from
the estate of Lucian Freud and
allocated to the Scottish National
Gallery, 2013

This lively, spirited portrait was the only work by Constable that Freud owned and one of the last paintings he bought, in 2008. Freud had, by his own admission, 'only arrived at Constable progressively', yet the sympathy he felt for the work of the earlier artist was profound, dating back to his time as an art student in Dedham, in 'Constable country'. It culminated six decades later with his involvement in a major Constable exhibition held in Paris in 2002. Freud, whose relationship with museums was long-standing, had previously curated an exhibition for the National Gallery in London that included works by Constable. Among the pictures he selected for the Paris show were several portraits, an aspect of Constable's production hitherto considered secondary to his landscapes, yet one Freud particularly praised. He valued their sincerity, lack of sophistication and quintessential Englishness. Here, a pale winter light falls on the diaphanous skin of Constable's young model; her vivacious face is rendered with remarkable sensitivity, using a sober palette of silvery whites and grey. AR

Henri Matisse

6 | Henri Matisse
Self Portrait, 1918
Oil on canvas, 65 × 54 cm
Musée d'Orsay, Paris, dépôt au
musée départemental Henri Matisse,
Le Cateau-Cambrésis, donation de
Mme Jean Matisse, 1979

Well aware of the art historical
precedents, Matisse (1869–1954)
painted numerous pictures of an
artist at work in the studio. Only
four are actual self portraits. This,
the last, was started in December
1917, a few days after his arrival in
Nice. Confined to his hotel room
by bronchitis and persistent rain,
surrounded by simple objects,
Matisse paints his reflection in
his wardrobe mirror: a calm,
introspective image, in which the
tight orthogonal composition,
characteristic of the formal
investigations of his earlier years,
is imbued with a new serenity. He
concentrates on the material texture
of objects – here delineated with
black lines around areas of colour
– a quality he also looked for in
the paintings he bought, such as
Degas's *Combing the Hair* (cat. 12).
Having barely completed this self
portrait, Matisse took it, and on a
different visit the Cézanne opposite,
to the elderly Renoir in nearby Cagnes,
seeking approval from another
master whose influence on his own
work would prove essential. AR

7 | **Paul Cézanne**
Three Bathers, 1879–82
Oil on canvas, 55 × 52 cm
Petit Palais, Musée des
Beaux-Arts de la Ville de Paris

Three Bathers is a landmark in the history of modern art. The fundamental impact on Matisse's art, both formal and emotional, of this intensely energetic canvas cannot be overstated, from the seminal moment of its purchase in 1899, which was a major financial sacrifice for the Matisse household. Matisse was magnetically drawn to the picture, obsessed by it even before he came to own it, recalling how, in the few weeks before purchasing it, taking walks in the countryside, he 'kept seeing his Cézanne'. Matisse venerated it, waking up before dawn to contemplate the picture lit by the first rays of the sun: absorbing its uncompromising modernity while using it as a yardstick by which to measure his own work. A talisman, providing stimulus as well as reassurance, it also soothed his creative anxiety: 'In the thirty-seven years I have owned this canvas', he wrote in 1936, '… it has sustained me morally in the critical moments of my venture as an artist; I have drawn from it my faith and my perseverance.' AR

8 | **Paul Gauguin**
Young Man with a Flower behind his Ear, 1891
Oil on canvas, 45.4 × 33.5 cm
Property from a distinguished private collection – courtesy of Christie's

Bought from Vollard in 1900 before he could afford such a purchase, Matisse had to pay for this work by Gauguin in several instalments. He even, according to one account, pawned his wife's ring – his wedding gift to her – to be able to acquire it. As Yve-Alain Bois put it, the picture 'unmistakeably evokes Matisse's own works without it being possible to say exactly why', maybe due to 'the touching strangeness of the flower on the young man's ear'. The sitter is believed to be Gauguin's friend Jotépha, described by the artist as a 'young man, very simple and very handsome', whom he encountered on his first trip to Tahiti in 1891. He is here adorned with the traditional *tiaré* – Tahitian gardenia, creamy-white and fragrant – which contrasts with his Western shirt and cravat. Matisse was undoubtedly attracted to the primitivism of the portrait, its rich colours, flattened forms and simplified lines. However, he parted with it in 1915, having previously attempted to exchange it in 1908 for a work by Renoir, whose pictures of indolent women intrigued him increasingly: an indication of the evolution of his taste. AR

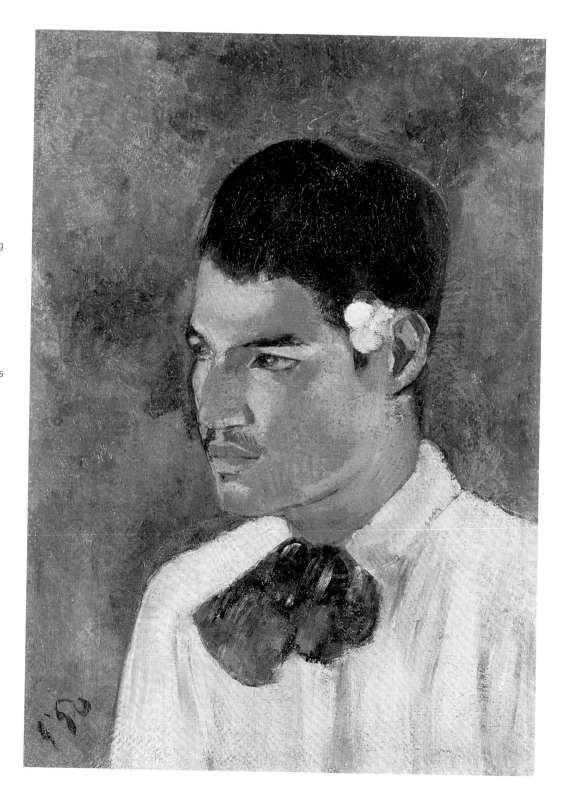

9 | **Paul Signac**
The Green House, Venice
(*La maison verte, Venise*), 1905
Oil on canvas, 46 × 55.2 cm
Private collection

Staying in Venice in the spring of 1904, Signac was mesmerised by the coloured sailing boats and shimmering reflections of light on the lagoon. Although painted back in his studio at Saint-Tropez, this picture conveys his sense of wonder, while demonstrating his rigorous mastery of the Neo-Impressionist programme: a theory based on divided colour and the scientific method Signac promoted tirelessly. Among his converts was Matisse, who, staying with Signac the following summer, briefly adopted this style, but also acquired a painting in the idiom: this work, which Matisse selected in lieu of payment for his own canvas *Luxe, calme et volupté* – his declaration of divisionist allegiance – which Signac chose to decorate his dining room. Stimulated by Signac's intense colour and enlarged, mosaic-like touch, by the time Matisse acquired this painting his style was evolving in yet another direction, that of Fauvism. Still, his interest in the technique did not wane; 10 years later he purchased a small, forcefully divisionist study by Seurat, of dazzling chromatic intensity: *Moored Boats and Trees* (1890, Philadelphia Museum of Art). AR

10 | **Henri Matisse**
Portrait of Greta Moll, 1908
Oil on canvas, 93 × 73.5 cm
The National Gallery, London

The German painter and sculptor
Greta Moll sat for this portrait a few
months after joining the art academy
Matisse had founded in Paris in 1907,
where she was the youngest of the
10 inaugural students. As part of his
teachings Matisse would take his
pupils to his studio to show them the
objects and pictures he had been
collecting for more than a decade:
'veritably festive afternoon hours',
as one student recalled, which
culminated in the contemplation of
Cézanne's *Three Bathers* (cat. 7).
Matisse's assimilation of Cézanne's
pictorial concerns is certainly manifest
in this portrait, striking for its simple
solidity and daring plasticity, which
the sitter found disconcerting, if
not 'disastrous'; it took several
decades for Greta to be won over
by her 'painter's painting'. The vivid
flowered cotton fabric behind her
statuesque figure was another of
Matisse's venerated possessions:
a bold, arresting piece of 'toile de
Jouy' that he had bought a few years
earlier, and one of the highlights in
the collection of textiles he was also
forming: the 'little museum of fabrics',
which he valued hardly less than
his paintings. AR

11 | **Paul Cézanne**
Madame Cézanne, 1886–7
Oil on canvas, 46.8 × 38.9 cm
Philadelphia Museum of Art:
The Samuel S. White 3rd and
Vera White Collection, 1967

Cézanne's wife, Hortense Fiquet, was his most frequently painted model, yet not a conventional muse. Detached and impassive, she is here observed with a psychological distance combined with emotional intensity. The portrait's strangeness is emphasised by the severe geometry of Hortense's face, her head slightly tilted, accentuating the sharp line of her jaw. This is one of two portraits of Madame Cézanne that Matisse came to own, maybe not simultaneously; he might have traded it at the dealer Paul Rosenberg in 1918 for a slightly later and equally disconcerting likeness (1888–90, Musée d'Orsay). Matisse briefly encountered the elderly Madame Cézanne a few years afterwards, during a dinner with Renoir's son Jean. Curiously, however, Matisse had never attempted to meet Cézanne himself, this 'kind of God of painting', in his own words. Crushed under his daunting tutelage, Matisse may have consciously avoided him, arguing that 'an artist is wholly in his production'. AR

12 | **Hilaire-Germain-Edgar Degas**
Combing the Hair ('La Coiffure'),
about 1896
Oil on canvas, 114.3 × 146.7 cm
The National Gallery, London
(detail, p. 40)

This everyday scene framed by a heavy velvet curtain never left Degas's studio during his life. It was considered for acquisition by the National Gallery in 1918, but rejected for being too coarse. Undeterred, Matisse bought it soon after and did not part with it until 1936, when he entrusted his son Pierre, the New York art dealer, to sell it for him. Kenneth Clark, then Director of the National Gallery, bought it on a visit to Pierre Matisse's gallery, while actually looking for a Matisse for himself. Matisse reacted to the news of the sale with a frustratingly succinct 'Good for this Degas'. Puzzlingly, in the 16 years he owned this painting – his only work by Degas – Matisse does not seem to have displayed it, or commented on it; yet his own paintings are an unquestionable tribute to Degas's radical use of intense oranges and reds, his attention to textiles and textures, and his unrivalled sense of casual intimacy. AR

13 | **Henri Matisse**
| *The Inattentive Reader*
| (*La liseuse distraite*), 1919
| Oil on canvas, 73 × 92.4 cm
| Tate

Matisse was spending his third consecutive winter in Nice when early in 1919 he painted this image of a distracted reader – the professional model is Antoinette Arnoud – in his room at the Hôtel de la Méditerranée overlooking the limpid sea. He was very much interested in depicting interiors and the natural light playing across their spaces during his time in Nice, and no less intrigued by the representation of women caught up in their own thoughts and actions, largely oblivious of those who observe them. His fascination with audacious colour was by now a constant.

It was about this time that he added to his small but select collection of paintings by admired contemporaries and predecessors Degas's *Combing the Hair* (opposite). This late work intersects with all of Matisse's prevailing artistic concerns and suggests what he looked for in the pictures he collected, and the kind of inspiration he drew from them. CR

14 | (this page)
Pablo Picasso
Portrait of a Woman: Dora Maar,
20 January 1942
Gouache on paper, 40.5 × 30.3 cm
Private collection, United Kingdom

15 | (opposite page)
Pablo Picasso
Portrait of Dora Maar, 1942
Oil on canvas, 61.6 × 50.5 cm
Courtesy The Elkon Gallery,
New York City

Since their encounter in the fertile first decade of the twentieth century, when both artists were laying the very foundations of modern art, Matisse and Picasso began to exchange pictures. Fascinated as well as stimulated by their extraordinary variety of styles, they seized on the lessons they could learn from each other, if only to reject them; beyond their temperamental differences, they always remained preoccupied with their rival's ever-evolving investigations. 'Picasso shatters forms,' Matisse declared, 'I am their servant.'

This complicated relationship eased with time; Picasso presented these two works to the elderly Matisse probably in 1942 and 1943, an amicable gesture towards the convalescing artist. Both depict Picasso's lover Dora Maar, her face dramatically distorted, volume conferred through the play of light on her jagged, angular features. The painting opposite shows her majestic against a solid grey background, prompting Matisse to exclaim: 'It's Dante before Hell ... What magic!' Matisse displayed it on the wall of his apartment at the Hôtel Régina in Nice, above a ceramic owl vase by Picasso. By then he had largely parted with his collection of pictures – by Cézanne, Degas, Courbet, artists whom Picasso also eagerly collected – but had retained his works by Picasso. Living with them, Matisse was constantly reminded of Picasso's challenge, perpetuating what has remained one of art history's most creatively dynamic exchanges. AR

Edgar Degas

16 | **Hilaire-Germain-Edgar Degas**
Self Portrait, 1855
Oil on paper laid on canvas,
81.3 × 64.5 cm
Musée d'Orsay, Paris

Degas (1834–1917) produced this austere work, one of his most accomplished self portraits, before the age of 21. It is, however, a surprisingly mature image, demonstrating the knowledge of the art of the past that would underpin his whole oeuvre. During his formative years Degas copied the Old Masters extensively. Here, his charcoal holder in one hand, Degas presents himself as a draughtsman; his other hand rests on a portfolio, probably containing his numerous copies and studies after the artists he most revered.

Years later, when Degas started collecting pictures, he sought works related to those he had admired and copied as a young man, such as Ingres's *Angelica saved by Ruggiero* (cat. 18). He also acquired a number of portraits by Ingres. Ingres's influence is evident in this self portrait, painted shortly after Degas had met him for the first time. Degas may have reworked it in about 1895, perhaps under the influence of the paintings by Ingres that he owned and was at leisure to contemplate. AR

17 | **Jean-Auguste-Dominique Ingres**
Monsieur de Norvins, 1811–12
Oil on canvas laid down on panel,
97.2 × 78.7 cm
The National Gallery, London

Norvins was one of those ambitious provincial Frenchmen who early on embraced the upstart Napoleon Bonaparte. Entering the future Emperor's service in 1797, he proved himself an able administrator and was named Chief of Police for the Roman States in 1810. He arrived in Rome at the beginning of 1811 and, full of his own importance, sat to Ingres later that same year. The writer Stendhal found Norvins 'truly wicked', and more than one comparison has been made over the years with Puccini's depraved Roman police chief Scarpia in the opera *Tosca*.

Degas passionately admired Ingres's portraits – paintings and drawings both – his collection including five of the former. He purchased *Monsieur de Norvins* from the dealer Haro in 1898. The National Gallery acquired it at the posthumous auctions of Degas's collection in 1918. CR

18 | Jean-Auguste-Dominique Ingres
Angelica saved by Ruggiero,
1819–39
Oil on canvas, 47.6 × 39.4 cm
The National Gallery, London

The subject comes from Ludovico Ariosto's epic poem *Orlando Furioso* (1516) and shows the hero Ruggiero, mounted on a fantastical beast, rescuing the vulnerable and contorted heroine. Ingres first treated the theme on a large scale in 1819 (Musée du Louvre, Paris) and, perhaps because it allowed him to depict variants of one of his most ravishing female nudes, returned to it on several occasions. This enamel-like rendering of uncertain date made its way into the collection of one of Ingres's closest friends, Frédéric Reiset, who as curator of drawings and then of paintings at the Louvre, and finally as director of the Musées de France, was a highly esteemed connoisseur. Degas would have been conscious of this distinguished provenance, and of the personal connection with the infinitely admired Ingres, when, Reiset having died in 1891, his collection came up for auction in 1894 and was bought by Degas. At an unknown date Degas also acquired an exquisite, early drawing of the same composition (Harvard University Art Museums, Cambridge, MA). CR

19 | Jean-Auguste-Dominique Ingres
Dante offering his Works to Homer (study for
The Apotheosis of Homer), about 1827 and about 1864–5
Oil on three pieces of canvas mounted on wood, 38 × 35.5 cm
Ordrupgaard, Copenhagen

The Italian poet Dante's distinctive profile is instantly recognisable. The work began as a study for a detail of the monumental allegory Ingres undertook in 1825 to decorate a ceiling at the Musée du Louvre, *The Apotheosis of Homer*. Years later, again at work on the theme, Ingres seems to have united earlier sketches for the poet's face and for his right hand on a third piece of canvas, to which he added the left hand, the book and perhaps the laurel wreath. It is in effect a collage.

Degas seems to have acquired the painting at auction in Paris in 1897. It is one of 21 drawings and oil sketches related to Ingres's decorative painting, which he purchased whenever the opportunity arose. Degas considered *The Apotheosis of Homer* to be a pinnacle of French art of the nineteenth century by a master whose skills as a draughtsman and endless invention with multi-figure compositions he worshipped. CR

20 | Jean-Auguste-Dominique Ingres
Pindar and Ictinus, probably 1830–67
Oil on canvas laid down on panel,
34.9 × 27.9 cm
The National Gallery, London

Pindar was an ancient Greek lyric poet – hence the lyre he holds aloft – while Ictinus, architect's rule in hand, designed the Parthenon in Athens. Both appear in Ingres's *The Apotheosis of Homer* completed in 1827 (Musée du Louvre, Paris). Another of the many studies for that monumental work that Degas assiduously collected, it began as a sketch but decades later was turned into the small, finished work we see today. Intended for sale, it was executed at the time Ingres

returned to the theme late in life to prepare a large multi-figure drawing entitled *Homer Deified* (also Musée du Louvre).

Degas acquired the work on the Paris market in 1898. Ictinus, in shadow and full-face, plays far less prominent a role than the poet, seen in classic profile. Indeed, Degas seems to have been particularly drawn to Ingres's mastery of the painted profile; he would come to own seven such studies by the artist. CR

21 | **Eugène Delacroix**
Louis-Auguste Schwiter, 1826–30
Oil on canvas, 217.8 × 143.5 cm
The National Gallery, London

Baron Schwiter, a young dandy exquisitely turned out in sober British dress, was an artist friend and distant relation of Delacroix, and the subject of one of his most elegant full-length portraits. Indebted to the 'swagger' portraits of Lawrence, whom Delacroix admired and had visited in London in 1825, it is an exercise in the anglophilia that he and Schwiter shared with stylish contemporaries in artistic Parisian circles. Another painter friend, Paul Huet, may have assisted Delacroix by painting the English garden against which Schwiter is silhouetted.

Degas acquired the painting in 1895 and gave it a prominent place in his collection. It was one of 15 oil paintings by Delacroix that he owned, along with numerous works on paper, and it hung adjacent to similarly refined portraits by Ingres. It was bought by the National Gallery at the posthumous Degas sales in Paris of 1918, reportedly in lively bidding against the Louvre. CR

22 Eugène Delacroix
Hercules rescuing Hesione, 1852
Oil on canvas, 24.5 × 47.5 cm
Ordrupgaard, Copenhagen

This sketch is a study for one of several lunettes recounting the life of Hercules in the Salon de la Paix of the Hôtel de Ville, Paris; all were destroyed by fire during the 1871 Commune. By then this painting had been in a posthumous auction of Delacroix's studio effects in February 1864, and was soon purchased by the pioneering collector Victor Chocquet. Renoir included it in the background of his 1875 portrait of Chocquet (Harvard University Art Museums, Cambridge, MA).

Chocquet's collection was dispersed at auction in 1899. Degas was there to snap up this sketch and another, evidence of an interest in Delacroix's working methods that had been heightened by the publication in 1893 of the artist's *Journal*, which he read – or rather, such was his eyesight, he had read to him – avidly. Degas's fascination was partly with Chocquet himself; he would go on to acquire one of Cézanne's portraits of the eccentric collector as well (about 1877, Virginia Museum of Fine Arts, Richmond, VA). CR

23 | (above)
Eugène Delacroix
Study of the Sky at Sunset,
1849–50
Pastel and coloured chalk on
blue paper, 22.8 × 26.8 cm
The British Museum, London

24 | (below)
Hilaire-Germain-Edgar Degas
Study of a Sky (*Etude de Ciel*),
about 1869
Pastel on grey-blue paper,
29 × 48 cm
Musée d'Orsay, Paris

Delacroix's radiant pastel is one of
several studies of sunlit or cloudy
skies that the artist executed
around 1850. It was probably made
on the Normandy coast, with its
characteristically soft, changeable
light. This is a radically bare,
simple image, very different to the
emotionally charged paintings, based
on historic and literary scenes full of
violent action and chaotic figures,
for which Delacroix is celebrated.
It nonetheless appealed to Degas,
who was fascinated by every aspect
of Delacroix's oeuvre, and who
acquired a large number of works by
the older painter. Delacroix's mastery
of pastel was of particular interest to
Degas, who became a virtuoso in this
medium, exploring the full potential
of its textures and colours.

Degas was no doubt stimulated by
the expressive draughtsmanship and
romantic sensibility of Delacroix's
Study of the Sky at Sunset. Using just
a few streaks of orange and blue,
Delacroix created the impression of
a light haze with extraordinary ease.
Degas probably produced his *Study
of a Sky* in the summer of 1869, also
on the Normandy coast. Much like in
Delacroix's pastel, the vast expanse
of sky is divided into several
luminous zones, rendered in a few
feathery layers of pastel. In these
works both artists excel at evoking
the fugitive clouds and unique
atmosphere of the seaside. AR

25 | **Jean-Baptiste-Camille Corot**
The Roman Campagna, with the
Claudian Aqueduct, probably 1826
Oil on paper laid on canvas, 22.8 × 34 cm
The National Gallery, London

Degas bought *The Roman Campagna*, along with a painting by Rousseau, at Comte Armand Doria's sale in 1899. It was one of seven pictures by Corot (of which six were landscapes) owned by Degas, who greatly admired his work – particularly, and unusually for the time – his early Italian views. He was probably attracted to them because of his own time spent in Italy in the 1850s, of which he wrote: 'A feeling of antiquity survives in the countryside, that is wild, empty, cursed like the desert, with its great mountains carrying aqueducts and its herds of cattle spread far and wide. This is really beautiful, with the kind of beauty that is like a dream of antiquity.'

Fragments of the Roman Claudian aqueduct, which lay just to the south of Rome, are strung out across the sunlit plain. The medieval Tour Fiscale holds centre stage, linking the fluidly painted landscape with the bright sky laden with majestic clouds. SH

26 | **Camille Pissarro**
| *Landscape at Pontoise*, 1872
| Oil on canvas, 46 × 55 cm
| The Ashmolean Museum, Oxford

Under a still grey sky a path draws the eye into an extensive rural landscape. On the right labourers ride on a hay-laden cart, diminutive figures dwarfed by the land. From 1866 to 1883 Pissarro spent prolonged periods living and working in Pontoise, to the north-west of Paris, where he produced numerous views of its cultivated fields, gardens and factories. Here, the even light, path and repoussoir tree on the left all recall the work of Corot, a landscapist who was immensely influential on the Impressionists during their formative years, particularly on Pissarro, who worked alongside the older artist.

Degas often professed a dislike of the countryside, yet his collection contained a sizeable number of landscapes. While involved with the Impressionist group exhibitions in the 1870s, he acquired several paintings by his contemporaries soon after they were completed, including this one and two others by Pissarro, who 'could not be more flattered' at Degas's attention and support. SH

27 | **Alfred Sisley**
The Flood. Banks of the Seine,
Bougival, 1873
Oil on canvas, 50 × 65.5 cm
Ordrupgaard, Copenhagen
(detail, p. 52)

The Seine to the west of Paris was in flood from December 1872 and for several weeks Sisley found compelling landscape motifs along its swollen banks. Here he portrays an austere factory building at Bougival, not yet inundated but isolated by the rising waters. Smoke from a chimney to the left suggests that work bravely carries on.

Signed and dated '73, the painting was acquired by Degas that same year. It was Degas's only work by Sisley – was it a gift from the artist? – and one of very few 'classic' Impressionist landscapes in his collection. There were three landscapes by Pissarro, one by Morisot and nothing at all, not even a sketch, by Monet. Among the core Impressionist group only his dear friend Cassatt was well represented but then, like Degas, she was primarily a figure painter. CR

28 | Edouard Manet
Woman with a Cat, about 1880–2
Oil on canvas, 92.1 × 73 cm
Tate

The sitter is Suzanne Leenhoff, Manet's wife and the subject of several of his portraits. Unfinished, the canvas reveals Manet's working method in building up forms with a distinctive hatching brushstroke that serves to differentiate areas of light and shade. At the same time the close-up viewpoint and informal pose, left hand lifted to brow, not to mention the sleeping cat, impart a compelling sense of domestic intimacy – the setting is the family apartment in the rue de Saint-Pétersbourg – which the very lack of finish further emphasises.

Over the years Degas acquired nine paintings by his dear friend Manet, one of which, a gift, he returned in a fit of pique. He obtained *Woman with a Cat* in 1894 from the dealer Vollard, paying for it with one of his own pastels. After Degas's death, the painting was bought for the nation at the 1918 sales. CR

29 | **Georges Jeanniot**
Conscripts (Conscrits), 1894
Oil on canvas, 72.7 × 86.3 cm
Collection of Ömer Koç

Degas collected masterpieces by the nineteenth-century painters Ingres and Delacroix, but he also bought work by his immediate contemporaries, such as this picture, purchased a year after its completion for a significant price. The painting, which shows a group of naked conscript soldiers being put through a fitness test, would have intrigued Degas, who had a lifelong preoccupation with the representation of the nude. The awkward poses of the boys shivering in the cold, bare room echo Degas's own research into the human figure, as attested by his *Young Spartans Exercising* (National Gallery, London, about 1860), a major early work depicting naked girls and boys engaged in a wrestling contest.

Jeanniot served in the army before embarking on a career as a successful draughtsman and illustrator. He was an astute observer of modern life, and counted Manet and Degas among his friends (often entertaining Degas at his country house in Burgundy). *Conscripts* is a token of their friendship. Long thought lost, the painting reappeared at auction in 2014. AR

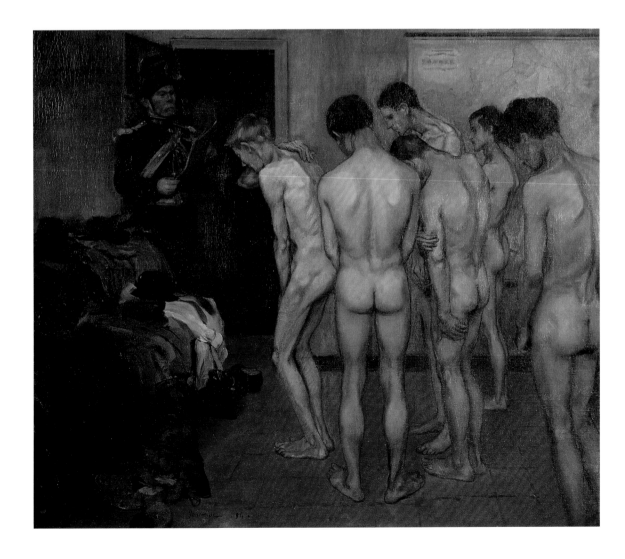

30 | **Edouard Manet**
The Execution of Maximilian,
about 1867–8
Oil on canvas, four fragments
mounted, 193 × 284 cm
The National Gallery, London

One of Manet's most ambitious history paintings, the *Execution* exists in four versions painted soon after the event depicted and seemingly intended as a provocation to the French government, which had failed to support the Austrian archduke it had imposed on Mexico as emperor. One version was soon ordered off public display in Paris. This version remained with Manet, was damaged perhaps by water, cut up posthumously and unceremoniously dispersed around Paris. Motivated by admiration for his old friend, Degas set out to reassemble what pieces he could find, four in the end. They do not include Maximilian himself; we see only his left hand grasping that of one of the two loyal generals with whom he faced the firing squad. The wonder is that the National Gallery purchased this magnificent ruin – but ruin nonetheless – at the Degas sales of 1918, its very first but surprisingly unhesitant foray into the acquisition of modern art. CR

31 | **Jacques-Emile Blanche**
  Francis Poictevin, 1887
  Oil on canvas, 26.7 × 16.5 cm
  Tate

Degas was not an easy friend. He was prone to take offence and when he did so reacted with peremptory disdain. The society painter Blanche, famous for his inexhaustible charm, discovered this when he allowed a portrait he had painted of the artist in about 1903 (North Carolina Museum of Art, Raleigh) to be reproduced in a magazine without Degas's permission. To Degas's fury, the image seemed to reveal to the public his failing eyesight. Blanche was an old friend but, silently, Degas returned to him this portrait, which he had owned for many years. Still feeling the sting years later, Blanche ruefully recalled that it had even hung in Degas's bedroom.

The work shows the Symbolist writer Poictevin, a model for the aesthete Jean des Esseintes in Joris-Karl Huysmans's decadent novel, *A Rebours* (1884). Blanche's portrait succinctly reveals his skills with elegant contours and with the evocation of psychological presence. CR

32 | **Paul Gauguin**
A Vase of Flowers, 1896
Oil on canvas, 64 × 74 cm
The National Gallery, London

As he grew older, Degas kept a lively eye on the coming generation of painters, many of whom were struggling financially, encouraging them and even buying works when sending a bit of money their way might have helped. Cézanne and Van Gogh figured precociously in his collection. He was especially intrigued by the intensification of colour the young artists were exploring and here Gauguin in particular benefited from the old man's enthusiasm.

Indeed, Ann Dumas has described the relationship between the two as that of mentor and protégé. Degas would come to own no fewer than 11 brilliantly hued Gauguin canvases, including this exuberant Tahitian flower piece, which he bought from the artist's friend and Paris agent Daniel de Monfreid in June 1898. It is justified to speculate on the impact of such paintings on Degas's own late works where the use of strong colours is a defining characteristic. CR

33 | **Paul Cézanne**
Bather with Outstretched Arm
(study), 1883–5
Oil on canvas, 33 × 24 cm
Collection Jasper Johns

The pioneering dealer Vollard opened the first solo exhibition ever of works by Cézanne in his tiny Paris gallery in November 1895. Degas was there and on 20 November bought this odd, angular and psychologically ambiguous painting of a standing male bather. Seemingly unsteady on his feet, the boy is lost in private reverie. Small as the canvas is, the painting is monumental in conception and encapsulates the artist's experiments with the bathing figure, both male and female, from the mid-1870s to the end of his life. Degas would come to own at least eight works by Cézanne.

Perhaps it is not surprising that a work that would appeal to one, deeply questioning painter should appeal to another. From Degas's collection, the *Bather* later passed to that of the great American painter, Jasper Johns, for whom Cézanne has been a primary point of reference throughout his long career. CR

Frederic, Lord Leighton

34 | **Frederic, Lord Leighton**
Self Portrait, 1882
Oil on canvas, 34.5 × 29.7 cm
Aberdeen Art Gallery
& Museums Collections

Leighton (1830–96) painted or drew fewer than 10 self portraits. This one was commissioned by the Scottish collector Alexander Macdonald, who supplied the stretched canvas. Leighton may have felt constrained by its relatively small size. Poised, slightly aloof, he depicted himself wearing the distinctive white smock and red cravat characteristic of late nineteenth-century studios, his loosely arranged grey curls creating an informal effect. Set against the vibrant background of a lightly brushed curtain, he looks pensively out of the picture, in a semi-oblique pose, bathed in soft sunlight. The painting harks back to Renaissance self portraits well known to Leighton. Having studied and copied the works of the Old Masters during his formative years on the Continent, Leighton later appropriated them – in a physical sense – by buying their pictures, assembling a collection of note. He displayed them in the extravagantly refined setting of his studio house at Holland Park, among a magnificent array of objects including Middle-Eastern pottery, rugs and tapestries. AR

35 | **Eugène Delacroix**
The Muse of Orpheus, 1845–7
Pen and ink heightened with oil on
paper, laid on canvas, 21.3 × 25.5 cm
The Syndics of the Fitzwilliam Museum,
Cambridge

In 1840 Delacroix received a prestigious commission to decorate the Library of the French Senate in the Palais du Luxembourg, Paris. A central dome shows ancient Greek and Roman exemplars of good government. The dome's four pendentives feature attendant figures, including the muse of Orpheus, sketched here with remarkable concision. Following Delacroix's death in 1863 a sale of his studio effects in February of the following year, including hundreds of such sketches, allowed even enthusiasts of little means to acquire works by the master. Delacroix's renown among artists and connoisseurs spread.

Leighton was at the Paris sale to scoop up this sketch. Surely he was impressed by Delacroix's freedom of execution and mastery of the classical idiom he himself explored. It was included in the posthumous auction of Leighton's own collection, in 1896, and there it was purchased by two more artists of high aesthetic leaning, Charles Ricketts and Charles Shannon. CR

36 Jean-Baptiste-Camille Corot
The Four Times of Day, about 1858
Oil on wood, *Morning* 142.2 × 72.3 cm;
Noon 142.2 × 62.2 cm; *Evening* 142.2 × 72.3 cm;
Night 142.2 × 64.7 cm
The National Gallery, London

Four different landscapes trace the day's progress from glowing dawn to starry night, each framed by tall graceful trees. Small figures enliven each view, some wearing red caps as foils to the dominant greens and browns. A prolific painter of decorative schemes,

Corot executed this set for the Fontainebleau home of fellow artist Alexandre Decamps. Completing the panels in a week, the speed with which he painted caused his friend to exclaim, 'Not so fast, don't hurry yourself so, there is enough soup for a few more days.'

Leighton lived and worked in Paris in the 1850s, and had met both Corot and Decamps. In 1865 he acquired the panels at Decamps's sale. Bought for the studio house he was having built in Holland Park Road, London, they were hung with other landscapes in the drawing room, whose carefully contrived and complementary colour scheme of greens, blues and browns heralded the Aesthetic Interior. SH

37 | **Frederic, Lord Leighton**
Aynhoe Park, 1860s
Oil on canvas, 34.3 × 40.6 cm
Private collection, courtesy of
The Ashmolean Museum, Oxford

This stunning view of the grounds at Aynhoe Park in Oxfordshire captures the atmosphere of a spring day, with a light breeze agitating the grass, trees and foliage. A branch in the upper foreground directs the eye deep into the picture, towards the vast expanse of landscape unrolling majestically under the cloudy sky. Here, Leighton's predilection for subdued effects of light and his free handling of paint are at odds with the aesthetic of landscape painting that was predominant in England in the 1860s. Instead, he adopts the Continental landscape tradition he had observed in the work of Corot, which he admired intensely. Leighton had been aware of Corot since training in France and had met the older artist in Paris in the early 1860s. Fresh and tonal, *Aynhoe Park* testifies to Leighton's appreciation and understanding of Corot's work, demonstrating its effect on his own artistic practice and vision of landscape. AR

38 Frederic, Lord Leighton
Trees at Cliveden, 1880s
Oil on canvas, 42 × 28 cm
Private collection

This bold, confident study records a striking motif: the old yew tree at Cliveden, Buckinghamshire, with its thick roots and massive trunk rising sinuously from the ground. The distinctive vertical composition, unusual for a landscape, brings to mind Corot's *Four Times of Day* (cat. 36), which Leighton had acquired in 1865 and which held pride of place in his drawing room. Brilliantly effortless, the painting illustrates his absorption of Corot's compositional tricks: it is a rare instance of Leighton introducing a figure into a landscape study, and thus a clear reference to the peasants, signalled by their red clothes or hats, that Corot used unfailingly to animate his landscapes. Here a young woman seated in the tangle of roots of the ancient tree conveys a notion of scale; the characteristically bright accent of her red skirt against the browns and greens anchors the composition. This picture is also a painter's painting, having been owned by the artist Val Prinsep, Leighton's friend. AR

39 | **Possibly by Jacopo Tintoretto**
Jupiter and Semele, about 1545
Oil on spruce, 22.7 × 65.4 cm
The National Gallery, London

The subject is taken from Ovid's *Metamorphoses*. Semele, reclining on the right, was killed by Jupiter's thunder and lightning after she begged him to appear to her in his divine form. Although the painting now tends to be viewed as an independent artwork, *Jupiter and Semele* was probably originally conceived as a piece of furniture, perhaps a panel made for the front of a chest, or *cassonne*.

When *Jupiter and Semele* was acquired by the National Gallery at Lord Leighton's posthumous sale in 1896, it was believed to be by Andrea Schiavone. The 1898 *Descriptive Catalogue* published by the Gallery noted that: 'Tintoret[to] said of him [Schiavone] that he made up for the weakness of his drawing by the beauty of his colour, and that the painter was to blame who did not possess one of his works in his studio'. Leighton, who had acquired this work by 1876 and thus owned it for at least 20 years, was unknowingly heeding Tintoretto's advice. Leighton's collection comprised no less than 27 Old Master paintings, of which more than half were by or attributed to Venetian artists. The rich, sophisticated colouring of Leighton's own canvases and his sumptuous rendering of draperies are clearly indebted to his admiration – as well as his first-hand knowledge – of sixteenth-century Venetian art. HO'N

George Frederic Watts

40 | George Frederic Watts
Self Portrait in a Red Robe,
about 1853
Oil on canvas, 154.9 × 74.9 cm
Watts Gallery

On account of it size and theatrical
mode of representation, this may
be the most imposing and arresting
image that Watts (1817–1904) painted
of himself. Here the artist gives
personal insight, but also presents
himself to his public, wearing the
full-length, Italian-inspired gown
of a 'Venetian Senator' (a title by
which the painting is sometimes
known), in the guise of a lawyer or
cleric. His dress forms an integral
part of Watts's identity, alluding to
his own role as an artist, but also,
through play-acting, self-consciously
proclaiming himself as heir to the
great masters of the past. The
painting pays homage to their
guidance and inspiration, evoking
the magnificence of Venetian
colour, as well as the sophisticated
naturalism of the Florentine school.

Watts had learned his trade during
a four-year-long stay in Italy, copying
the Old Masters. He acquired, or was
given, a few examples of their work,
not least the majestic *Knight of
S. Stefano* (opposite), which he
rated particularly highly. AR

41 | **Probably by Girolamo Macchietti**
A Knight of S. Stefano, after 1563
Oil on wood, 209.5 × 121.2 cm
The National Gallery, London

This monumental Florentine portrait was given to the National Gallery in 1861 by Watts, who described it as a 'fine one'. Full-length, life-size sixteenth-century Tuscan portraits are certainly rare and this is a striking example of the genre. The sitter cuts an impressive figure, proudly wearing the cross of the military order of S. Stefano, which was founded in 1561 by the Grand Duke of Tuscany, Cosimo I de' Medici.

The authorship of the portrait has puzzled generations of art historians. When Watts gave it to the National Gallery, he believed it to be by Jacopo da Pontormo. By 1863 this attribution had been revised to Bronzino by Sir Charles Eastlake, Director of the Gallery. It has since been catalogued as Alessandro Allori, painter to the Medici court, and most recently attributed to Girolamo Macchietti. It is perhaps surprising that early National Gallery catalogue entries focused almost as much on the richly carved table as they did on the austere portrayal of the sitter. HO'N

42 | **George Frederic Watts**
| *Autumn*, 1901–3
| Oil on canvas, 134.6 × 73.7 cm
| Watts Gallery

Watts had his own architect-designed house, Limnerslease, built in 1890–1 in the village of Compton in Surrey. In his last years he painted a number of landscapes based on the countryside around the house, stating that 'The desire in me to paint landscape grows, I want to paint landscapes more and more.'

As a close neighbour and regular visitor to Leighton's home, Watts would have been familiar with Corot's *Four Times of Day* (cat. 36). Comparable in size and composition to Corot's panels, with tall, framing trees bleeding off on each side, *Autumn* similarly derives from a centuries-old tradition of decorative subjects drawing on cyclical themes. The technique, however, could not be more different. In contrast to Corot's speed of painting, Watts reworked his landscapes over a period of years, his constant retouching resulting in a dense surface and rich texture, combined here with vivid autumnal colours of greens and browns. SH

Sir Thomas Lawrence

43 | **Sir Thomas Lawrence**
Self Portrait, about 1825
Oil on canvas, 91 × 71.4 cm
Royal Academy of Arts, London

Started around 1825 and never finished, this self portrait records Lawrence's (1769–1830) reluctance to paint his own image, despite his professional success as one of the most highly sought-after portraitists of the day. Although according to anecdote it was 'commanded' by George IV, it never left Lawrence's studio, where he kept it hidden, never showing it to anyone.

George IV supposedly proposed that Lawrence, as President of the Royal Academy, depict himself in the same Doctor of Civil Law gown worn by his predecessor Reynolds in his self portrait (cat. 50), albeit without the corresponding cap 'for we will not recognise you without your bald head'. In the event Lawrence opted only for the latter, making a feature of his strongly-lit bald head emerging from the darkness, recalling Rembrandt's self portraiture. The result is an intimate and psychologically charged portrait made all the more enigmatic by virtue of the fact that Lawrence felt unable to finish it. AG

44 | Raphael
An Allegory ('Vision of a Knight'),
about 1504
Oil on poplar, 17.1 × 17.3 cm
The National Gallery, London

Lawrence's vast collection has acquired a legendary status for the sheer number of Old Master drawings it contained. The focus on drawings was in part financially motivated, but a good painting by Raphael – whom Lawrence had admired ever since he started out as a precocious teenage talent – was another matter. As Lawrence wrote to his art agent ahead of a major sale in Paris, 'In drawings I still ask for the preference – in pictures I do not expect it, nor can I afford to buy them, unless you meet with another Raphael, a case which would justify exertion.' This tiny but radiant picture – described by the German painter Johann David Passavant as 'an exquisite gem' – appears to have been just the sort of work Lawrence regarded worthy of such financial 'exertion'; it remained in his possession for 19 years. AG

45 | **Agostino Carracci**
A Woman borne off by a Sea God (?),
about 1599
Charcoal and white chalk (a grey
wash applied later over the whole)
on paper, 203.2 × 410.2 cm
The National Gallery, London

Together with *Cephalus carried off by Aurora in her Chariot*, also in the National Gallery, this is a working cartoon made in preparation for the painted ceiling of the Gallery in Palazzo Farnese in Rome. Commissioned by Cardinal Odoardo Farnese, the ceiling was largely painted by the Carracci brothers (Annibale and Agostino) with Ovidian subjects, primarily focusing on the loves of the gods. Executed in charcoal and white chalk on blue-grey paper, the design was transferred from the cartoon to the ceiling by pouncing, and numerous differences between the cartoon and painting exist. The Carracci were skilled and prolific draughtsmen, and their drawings were extremely popular among British artists from the early seventeenth through to the nineteenth century. Both National Gallery cartoons were owned by Lawrence who, acquiring them sometime after August 1813, understood they were by Annibale Carracci. Lawrence, an opinionated connoisseur, believed that the Bolognese school, led by the Carracci, was 'far superior to that of the Florentine'. HO'N

46 | Sir Anthony van Dyck
Carlo and Ubaldo see Rinaldo conquered by Love for Armida, 1634–5
Oil on wood, 57 × 41.5 cm
The National Gallery, London

The subject is taken from Torquato Tasso's *Gerusalemme Liberata* (*Jerusalem Delivered*) (1580), a poem that narrates the recovery of Jerusalem by Godfrey of Bouillon, leader of the First Crusade to the Holy Land. In this composition the Spanish-style helmets of two knights, Carlo and Ubaldo, can be seen protruding from a bush on the left side of the painting. The men have discovered their fellow knight Rinaldo stupefied by love in the lap of the sorceress Armida. It is probable that Van Dyck executed the painting in grisaille to assist an engraver, in this instance Pieter de Jode the Younger, with transforming the composition into a print. Monochrome pictures eased the printmaker's task of endowing black and white prints with the tonal qualities of paintings, and were of particular interest to artist collectors like Lawrence, who owned the painting from 1788 and kept it until his death.

The panel passed from Lawrence to Sir Robert Peel, and was bought by the National Gallery in 1871. HO'N

47 | **Guido Reni**
The Coronation of the Virgin,
about 1607
Oil on copper, 66.6 × 48.8 cm
The National Gallery, London

The copper support of this small devotional picture allowed Reni to capitalise on the luminous effects of his characteristically colourful palette. He was very interested in Marian iconography, and this composition, showing the Virgin Mary being crowned by angels while seated on a throne of clouds, combines elements of her Coronation, Glorification and Assumption.

Reni painted various versions of these subjects throughout his career, on both a large and small scale, as well as exploring the theme through his drawings. Indeed, Lawrence owned not only this painting but also an ink and wash drawing by Reni (National Galleries of Scotland, Edinburgh), which shares a number of compositional elements with this copper. Although we can only speculate as to the sequence in which Lawrence acquired these works, the relationship between them must surely have been a motivating factor for their purchase. AG

48 | **Follower of Rembrandt**
A Seated Man with a Stick,
perhaps 1675–1725
Oil on canvas, 137.5 × 104.8 cm
The National Gallery, London

In July 1797 Lawrence offered to sell
A Seated Man with a Stick to the
art patron and collector, Sir George
Beaumont, on the condition that he
could buy it back four years later.
This proviso is a testament to the
high regard in which Lawrence held
the painting. Beaumont refused
the artist's caveat and secured the
painting outright by purchasing it
for a higher price. The two men's
desire to possess the work certainly
had to do with its painterly qualities
as well as, no doubt, its attribution
to Rembrandt.

The painting is no longer
considered to be by the Dutch
master. X-ray images also reveal that
the composition now visible was not
the first on this canvas. Underneath
the seated man is an inverted
depiction of Christ on the Cross,
and faint indications of other figures.
It is probable that in the interest
of economy the artist or workshop
that made this work reused an
older canvas. HO'N

49 | Sir Thomas Lawrence
Sir Francis Baring, First Baronet,
John Baring and Charles Wall, 1806–7
Oil on canvas, 156 × 226 cm
Private collection

Lawrence's composition is a fresh and dynamic take on the tradition of group portraits of male friendship, kinship and collegiality that extended back to Titian, via the work of Reynolds and Van Dyck. This pedigree did not go unnoticed when the picture was exhibited at the Royal Academy of Arts, London, in 1807, the *Star* newspaper praising it as 'one of the best executed conversation pieces the English School has to boast of: in it Mr Lawrence has combined the rich stiles of Van Dyck and Sir Joshua Reynolds.' Although commissioned by Sir Francis Baring to accompany two existing group portraits by Reynolds and Benjamin West, whom Lawrence would later succeed as President of the Royal Academy, the painting was recognised by West as 'an advance in the Art'. AG

Sir Joshua Reynolds

50 | Sir Joshua Reynolds
Self Portrait, about 1780
Oil on panel, 127 × 101.6 cm
Royal Academy of Arts, London

Intended to hang in the Assembly Room of the Royal Academy of Arts, London, where Reynolds (1723–1792), as first President, delivered his famous *Discourses*, this self portrait digests visually, much as the *Discourses* did verbally, the lessons of the Old Masters Reynolds so admired. Reynolds presents himself with the self-assurance befitting his position, turning his head to face the viewer as he confidently rests his left hand on a console table upon which stands a bust of Michelangelo. The Renaissance master featured frequently in Reynolds's *Discourses* as a model of artistic greatness and the bust depicted is probably the plaster cast owned by Reynolds of the original by Daniele da Volterra. Reynolds maintained an extensive collection of prints and his pose here recalls that seen in an engraved portrait of the Flemish painter Adam de Coster by Van Dyck, Reynolds's eminent predecessor in the tradition of British portraiture. AG

51 | **Giovanni Bellini**
The Agony in the Garden,
about 1465
Egg on wood, 81.3 × 127 cm
The National Gallery, London

When *The Agony in the Garden* was in Reynolds's collection it was thought to be by Andrea Mantegna. This confusion is understandable: Mantegna, Bellini's brother-in-law, had painted the same subject about five years before. Bellini's *Agony in the Garden* might be interpreted as an act of homage to or competition with Mantegna. But regardless of the possible relationship between the two paintings, *The Agony in the Garden* was probably intended for private devotion. Bellini uses landscape and light to convey the emotional intensity of the night preceding Christ's arrest and crucifixion. Dawn is breaking and so, despite the events to come, the painting is fundamentally hopeful. It is likely to be the painting appearing as No. 48 in Reynolds's posthumous sale of 1795, where it was described as 'a picture of great antiquity, possessing much merit [...] a valuable specimen of the state of art at that period'. It may have been one of the earliest paintings Reynolds owned. HO'N

52 | **After Michelangelo**
Leda and the Swan, after 1530
Oil on canvas, 105.4 × 141 cm
The National Gallery, London

This is probably the version of the mythological subject of Leda's seduction by Zeus disguised as a swan that was a prize piece in Reynolds's collection. The picture is no longer attributed to Michelangelo, and the esteem in which Reynolds held it can now be taken as an example of his somewhat patchy reputation as a connoisseur, something noted even by his contemporaries. While Reynolds, via the *Morning Chronicle*, proudly described the *Leda* in 1791 as among 'the greatest curiosities in this nation', the collector Richard Payne Knight later claimed, after Reynolds's death, that there had been 'false Michael Angelos swarming in his collection; which he [Reynolds] certainly believed to be true.' For Knight, Reynolds was 'a remarkable instance' of the fact that 'even the best artists are not always the least fallible judges in their own art.' AG

53 | Jacopo Bassano
The Good Samaritan, about 1562–3
Oil on canvas, 102.1 × 79.7 cm
The National Gallery, London

Here Bassano illustrates the parable narrated by Jesus in the New Testament. The priest and Levite who have passed a badly beaten traveller retreat into the landscape. In contrast, the Samaritan cares for the man, bathing his wounds in oil and wine. Bassano shows the Samaritan in the act of lifting the traveller onto his horse. The city in the background is possibly Bassano, the artist's birthplace, north of Venice. The artist's inclusion of a recognisable place inserted the parable into the viewers' contemporary world, bestowing it with relevance and immediacy.

When the painting was bought by the National Gallery in 1856, it was stated that 'This noble study of colouring, full of dignity and feeling, is from the Collection of Sir Joshua Reynolds, who kept it always hanging in his studio'. The painting cannot be positively assigned to Reynolds before 1791. He owned 18 pictures by 'Bassano' in total, which reveals his admiration for Venetian art. HO'N

54 | **Rembrandt**
The Lamentation over the Dead Christ, about 1635
Oil on paper and pieces of canvas
mounted onto oak, 31.9 × 26.7 cm
The National Gallery, London

The dead Christ is shown surrounded by the weeping figures of the Virgin Mary and Mary Magdalene. In this highly complex composition, Rembrandt incorporates references to other scenes from Christ's Passion. The first part of the work is formed of an oil sketch on paper, which was then attached to a piece of canvas and extended. The composition was enlarged again after the canvas was pasted onto a panel. The later additions, notably the thieves and a thin strip along the bottom, might have been by an artist working under Rembrandt's direction. This grisaille oil sketch is closely related to his drawing of the same subject (opposite). Reynolds often acquired paintings to learn more about the technique of artists he admired. Here, he may have wanted to explore the connection between what he might have viewed as a preparatory drawing and a painting. In fact, it is uncertain as to whether Rembrandt worked on the drawing while executing the National Gallery work, before or after. Like the more complete work, the present drawing was enlarged in stages by Rembrandt. The painting and drawing were together in Reynolds's collection between 1791 and his death in 1792. HO'N

55 Rembrandt
Lamentation over the Dead Christ,
about 1634–5
Pen and brown ink and brown wash, with red
and perhaps some black chalk, reworked in
oils 'en grisaille'; on paper, 21.6 × 25.4 cm
The British Museum, London

56 **Sir Anthony van Dyck**
*Portrait of George Gage with Two
Attendants*, probably 1622–3
Oil on canvas, 115 × 113.5 cm
The National Gallery, London

This painting is now recognised as depicting the English diplomat and art agent George Gage being offered a sculpture, but when Reynolds owned it in the eighteenth century he believed it to represent Rubens and the sculptor Martinus van den Enden the Elder in the foreground (the man behind them was also latterly described as an artist). This was a significant distinction, for Reynolds saw in this picture both a portrait of a great painter of the previous century whom he much admired, and an image of artistic collegiality. It is telling that Reynolds regarded this painting as an example of 'Vandyck's first manner, when he imitated Rubens and Titian'; by combining stylistic elements of three undisputed masters, its appeal to the first President of the Royal Academy lay in part precisely in its status as a specimen of the artistic genealogy in which he sought to situate himself. It hung above the door to his drawing room, where it was much admired by other artists. AG

57 | **Style of Sir Anthony van Dyck**
The Horses of Achilles,
1635–45
Oil on canvas, 105.5 × 91.5 cm
The National Gallery, London

This is an enigmatic painting by an artist working in the style of Van Dyck, possibly Jan Boeckhorst. The inscription in the lower part reads 'equi/aquillis/ex Zephyro' (the horses of Achilles, born of Zephyr), suggesting that the scene depicts Xanthus and Balius, the immortal horses of Achilles. The head at the top right might represent the horses' sire, the wind god Zephyrus. The inscription may have been added later, perhaps to enhance the importance of the work by giving it a classical subject matter. When the painting was exhibited at the British Institution in 1815 it was intimated that Reynolds had added to the composition. It is indeed possible that the painting was originally left unfinished as a sketch and 'completed' in the eighteenth century, by the addition of a background, the landscape below and the wind god's head at the top right. HO'N

58 | Nicolas Poussin
The Adoration of the Shepherds,
about 1633–4
Oil on canvas, 97.2 × 74 cm
The National Gallery, London

Poussin illustrates two key episodes associated with the birth of Christ in this painting. The main scene shows the holy family with shepherds, an ox and an ass. In the background, the heavenly host announces Christ's birth to shepherds. The motif of the kneeling shepherd is taken from one of the kings in the fresco by Raphael, *The Adoration of the Magi*, in the Vatican Loggie. There is a similar figure of a woman carrying a basket of fruit in the tapestry of *The Healing of the Lame Man* after Raphael, again in the Vatican. These influences are logical when we consider that Poussin lived and worked in Rome.

Some 20 copies of this composition have been recorded, testifying to its popularity among patrons, painters and collectors. This version was probably intended for private devotion, but the circumstances of the commission are not known. It had entered Reynolds's collection by 1761. Reynolds is reported to have refused an offer of 350 pounds or guineas for the work, an indication of the high regard in which he held it. HO'N

59 Thomas Gainsborough
Girl with Pigs, 1781–2
Oil on canvas, 125.6 × 148.6 cm
From the Castle Howard Collection

Reynolds generally avoided buying the art of his contemporaries, but made a rare exception for Gainsborough's *Girl with Pigs*, which he purchased when it was exhibited at the Summer Exhibition at the Royal Academy of Arts, London, in 1782, described by a London newspaper as the best picture there. Reynolds's purchase of one of his rivals' works was widely regarded as a great gesture of magnanimity, commented upon as such by no less than Queen Charlotte and Dr Samuel Johnson. Gainsborough wrote to Reynolds to thank him, saying: 'I may truly say that I have brought my Piggs to a fine market.' Reynolds's relationship with the picture was, however, much more complicated. He is said to have found the girl depicted insufficiently beautiful and by 1790 he had sold the picture for three times what he had paid for it. His description of it as 'by far the best Picture he ever Painted or perhaps ever will' is in itself something of a backhanded compliment to Gainsborough. AG

Sir Anthony van Dyck

Van Dyck's (1599–1641) collection was referred to by contemporaries as his 'Cabinet de Titien', so dominated was it by the work of the sixteenth-century Venetian master. Exhibited alongside his studio and shown to patrons when paying visits, Van Dyck's Titians played an important role in the creation and promotion of his own self-image as a pre-eminent painter of his age, and most particularly as the heir of Titian, the artistic predecessor he revered above all others. It certainly had the desired effect on Jean Puget de la Serre, secretary to Marie de Médicis, who recorded the French Queen Mother's visit to Van Dyck in Antwerp in 1627 and concluded that Van Dyck surely shared in the Venetian master's glory, being the 'wonder' of the seventeenth century, just as Titian had been the 'ornament' of the sixteenth.

This self portrait is the consummate example of the significance of Titian in Van Dyck's self-image, having been selected by the artist as the portrait by which he would be represented in his own *Iconography* series of engraved portraits of prominent figures. It recalls strongly Titian's *Portrait of Gerolamo (?) Barbarigo* (opposite), which Van Dyck certainly would have known, at least through engravings if not possibly even owned (potentially No. 18 in the inventory of his collection) late in his life. From the penetrating gaze of the artist turning over his shoulder, one eye obscured in shadow, the other suspended in a piercing stare, to the exquisite rendering of the sumptuous fabric such a pose invites, this is a bravura homage to the Venetian master by his self-styled heir. AG

60 | **Sir Anthony van Dyck**
Self Portrait, about 1629
Oil on canvas, 80 × 61 cm
Private collection

61 | **Titian**
Portrait of Gerolamo (?) Barbarigo,
about 1510
Oil on canvas, 81.2 × 66.3 cm
The National Gallery, London

62 | **Titian**
The Vendramin Family, venerating a Relic of the True Cross, 1540–5
Oil on canvas, 206.1 × 288.5 cm
The National Gallery, London

Van Dyck's collection of Titians was characterised by the remarkably high concentration of portraits it contained, a genre in which both Titian and Van Dyck distinguished themselves, and in which Van Dyck is perhaps most indebted to his sixteenth-century predecessor. There are few more beautiful examples of Van Dyck's inspired adaptation of Titian's portraiture of sixteenth-century Venice to the context of seventeenth-century England than in his superb portrait of *Thomas Killigrew and William,*

Lord Crofts (?) (opposite). The delicate treatment of hair and opulent fabrics, subtle compositional dynamics in the almost rhythmic arrangement of hand gestures, and the refined silhouetting of physiognomy against the sky all recall *The Vendramin Family*. The latter canvas was the first painting listed in the inventory of Van Dyck's collection, and probably arrived in England, if not directly to his collection, in the late 1630s, around the time when he was painting the double portrait now in the Royal Collection. AG

Sir Anthony van Dyck
Thomas Killigrew and William,
Lord Crofts (?), 1638
Oil on canvas, 132.9 × 144.1 cm
The Royal Collection/
HM Queen Elizabeth II

Notes

1. J. Northcote, *The Life of Sir Joshua Reynolds*, 2nd edition [1819], vol. II, pp. 23–4, quoted in Reynolds 1945 (June), p. 133.

2. Matisse, Couturier and Rayssiguier 1993, p. 205.

3. Thirteen paintings were purchased by the National Gallery at the Degas sales in 1918, all from the first of the three collection sales. Among these, two were later transferred to the Tate Gallery: Forain, *The Tribunal*, about 1902–3 (N03288), and Manet, *Woman with a Cat*, about 1880–2 (N03295). Since 1997 the latter has been in the National Gallery on loan-term loan from the Tate (cat. 28), together with Blanche, *Francis Poictevin*, 1887 (L689), also from Degas's collection, acquired by the Tate Gallery in 1939 (cat. 31). In 1964 the National Gallery purchased another painting previously owned by Degas: Att. to Andrieu, *Still Life with Fruit and Flowers*, about 1850–64 (NG6349).

4. For instance Sir Edward Poynter, Director of the National Gallery between 1894 and 1904 and Leighton's successor as President of the Royal Academy, acquired *Jupiter and Semele* (cat. 39) attributed to Jacopo Tintoretto, from the sale in 1896, after Leighton's death. Poynter was also a painter, who had known Leighton for decades, having worked in the latter's studio in Rome during his years of training in the early 1850s.

5. Mary Cassatt, *Girl arranging her Hair*, 1886, National Gallery of Art, Washington, Chester Dale Collection; Degas, *Woman bathing in a Shallow Tub*, 1885, Metropolitan Museum of Art, New York. Cassatt kept the pastel for almost 33 years. See Dumas 1996, p. 10.

6. Bois 1998, p. 133.

7. Matisse, *Luxe, calme et volupté*, 1904, Musée d'Orsay, Paris.

8. Letter from Signac to Matisse, 1905. Archives Matisse, Issy-les-Moulineaux.

9. Dumas 1996, pp. 11–12, n. 53. To put this price into the context of the time, see Paris, London and Philadelphia 2014–15, p. 4.

10. London 1978, p. 70, n. 65–6. *Mrs Siddons as the Tragic Muse*, 1789, Private collection, cat. no. 1621, in Mannings and Postle 2000.

11. Eighteenth-century pastels inherited from his parents, an Aelbert Cuyp and two spectacular El Grecos. See Dumas 1996, p. 4.

12. Dumas 1996, p. 48.

13. Museum of Fine Arts, Boston.

14. For instance Renoir, *Dédée à la tasse de café*, 1917, Private collection; bought by Matisse soon after Renoir's death in 1919. See also Roger Benjamin, 'Pourquoi Matisse aimait-il le Renoir tardif?', in Paris, Los Angeles and Philadelphia, 2009–10, pp. 137–9 and Spurling 2005, p. 199.

15. Referred to as a 'Cabinet de Titien' not by Van Dyck, but by Puget de la Serre, secretary to Marie de Médicis, who visited Van Dyck in Antwerp in 1631. See Wood 1990, pp. 681 and 683.

16. Titian, *Perseus and Andromeda*, probably 1554–6, Wallace Collection, London.

17. Wood 1990, p. 683.

18. Ibid., p. 690.

19. Dumas 1996, pp. 23–4.

20. Archives du Musée d'Orsay, Fonds Degas-Fevre ODO 1996–31. Service de la Documentation, Musée d'Orsay.

21. See C. Grammont, 'Matisse collectionneur', in Martigny 2015, p. 195.

22. Letter from Félix Fénéon (galerie Bernheim-Jeune) to Matisse, 18 July 1908. Archives Matisse, Issy-les-Moulineaux.

23. J. Northcote, *The Life of Sir Joshua Reynolds*, 2nd edition [1819], vol. II, pp. 23–4, quoted in Reynolds 1945 (June), p. 133.

24. Paris in 1768 and 1771 (Thiers-Crozat sale, where Catherine the Great made substantial purchases); Flanders and Holland in 1781; Brussels in 1785. See London 1978, pp. 66–7.

25. See Twist 2006. The author of this essay is grateful to Dr Susanna Avery-Quash for drawing her attention to this book, and for her invaluable help.

26. Wood 1990, p. 681.

27. See Sickert 1917, p. 186.

28. Letter from A. Bartholomé to P. Lafond, 4 October 1896, in Dumas 1996, p. 14, n. 78.

29. New York 1997a, p. 24, n. 112.

30. Ingres, *Jacques-Louis Leblanc*, 1823, and *Madame Jacques-Louis Leblanc*, 1823, Metropolitan Museum of Art, New York.

31. Lapauze 1918, pp. 9–15.

32. Dumas 1996, p. 12, n. 54.

33. Ibid., p. 15, n. 87.

34. A. Alexandre, 'Le Marché aux toiles', *Le Figaro* (12 October 1901), p. 1.

35. Emmerich 1958, pp. 22–3.

36. Gertrude Stein, 1933, quoted in R.A. Rabinow, 'Vollard and Matisse', in New York, Chicago, Paris 2006–7, p. 133, n. 10.

37. Ibid.

38. Matisse claimed it to have been much embroidered by Gertrude Stein.

39. Spurling 1998, p. 180. Van Gogh, *Les Alyscamps*, 1888, Private collection, probably F 569 (see J.-B. de la Faille, *L'œuvre de Vincent van Gogh*, vol. 1 (Paris, 1928), p. 161).

40. Matisse bought the painting from Vollard together with Auguste Rodin's plaster bust of Henri Rochefort (not identified). See New York, Chicago and Paris, 2006–7, p. 131.

41. Escholier 1956, pp. 48–9.

42. 'Notre plus cher trésor', he said, referring to himself and his wife. The painting also became a symbol of family cohesion. In F. Turpin, *Elaboration de la collection privée d'Henri Matisse*, unpublished dissertation, Université de Paris IV Sorbonne 2002. Archives Matisse, Issy-les-Moulineaux.

43. Matisse, 'Notes d'un peintre', 1908, in Matisse 1972, p. 49.

44. Matisse, 'Notes d'un peintre', quoted in Rewald 1996, p. 239.

45. M. Weber, quoted in Baker 1987, p. 46, n. 2.

46. M. Weber, 'Cézanne and the crisis of art', in A. Barr, *Matisse: His Art and Public*, New York 1951, p. 87.

47. In the notes Reynolds compiled at the end of his life, in Broun 1987, p. 84.

48. Reynolds, *Fourteenth Discourse* (1788), in Wark 1959, p.256

49. 10 December 1778.

50. Rubens, *Landscape by Moonlight*, 1635–40, The Courtauld Gallery (Princes Gate Collection). See Braham and Bruce-Gardner 1988, p. 586.

51. Reynolds, *Discourses on Art*, in Wark 1959, p. 163. Quoted in Braham and Bruce-Gardner 1988, p. 586, fn 49.

52. Reynolds, 1769 *Discourse*.

53. Stourton and Sebag-Montefiore 2012, pp. 122–3.

54. L. Davis, 'Interacting with the Masters: Reynolds at the Wallace Collection', in London 2015a, p. 30.

55. Broun 1987, p. 82.

56. Reynolds, *Lord Rockingham and Edmund Burke*, about 1766, Fitzwilliam Museum, Cambridge. See B. Bryant, 'An Artist Collects: Leighton as a Collector of Painting and Drawings', in London 2010, p. 22.

57. London 1978, p. 72.

58. J. Northcote, *The Life of Sir Joshua Reynolds*, 2nd edition [1819], vol. II, p. 275, quoted in Reynolds 1945 (June), pp. 133–4. This was one of several aborted attempts by individuals or groups to encourage the establishment of a public art gallery in London.

59. 11–14 March 1795. See Reynolds 1945 (June), p. 133.

60. Eastlake writes he saw it 'long since' in a letter of 8 June 1861. Accepted by the National Gallery's Board of Trustees, 1 July 1861. Minutes, IV, 256, National Gallery Archives.

61. Letter to W.E. Gladstone, 25 June 1885, quoted in Gould 2004, p. 188. Watts also donated 18 of his Symbolist paintings to the Tate in 1897 (at the foundation of the National Gallery of British Art at Millbank) then more in 1900.

62. Dumas 1996, p. 19.

63. Degas lived there until 1912, when he moved to 6 boulevard de Clichy, where he was to remain until his death in 1917.

64. Sickert 1917, p. 186.

65. New York 1997a, p. 15.

66. Alexandre 1901, p. 1.

67. Wood 1990, p. 681.

68. New York 1997a, p. 20.

69. Ibid., pp. 17–191.

70. See fig. 7, in ibid., p. 10; photograph showing Degas's interior in the apartment rue Ballu, where he lived between 1890 and 1897.

71. London 2010, p. 70.

72. Bought for £3000 in the 1760s. Reynolds also owned a villa at Richmond.

73. L. Davis, 'Interacting with the Masters: Reynolds at the Wallace Collection', in London 2015a, p. 31.

74. Broun 1987, pp. 26–7.

75. Muller 1989, p. 68.

76. Wood 1990, p. 681, n. 10.

77. 1931. Archives Matisse, Issy-les-Moulineaux.

78. *Portrait of Suzanne Valadon*, about 1885, Private collection.

79. Ibid.

80. Letter from Matisse to Amélie, his wife, 23 June 1918. Archives Matisse, Issy-les-Moulineaux.

81. London 1978, pp. 68–9.

82. Garlick 1989, pp. 19–20.

83. Ormond 1975, p. 35.

84. Braham and Bruce-Gardner 1988, p. 592.

85. J. Northcote, *Memoirs of Sir Joshua Reynolds*, London, 1813, quoted in Braham and Bruce-Gardner 1988, p. 587, n. 57.

86. This is evident in another painting previously owned by Reynolds: Workshop of Velazquez, *Prince Baltasar Carlos in Black and Silver*, about 1640, Wallace Collection, London. See L. Davis, 'Interacting with the Masters: Reynolds at the Wallace Collection', in London 2015a, pp. 31–2.

87. London 1978, p. 69.

88. Matisse, *Portrait of Marguerite*, 1906–7, Musée Picasso, Paris.

89. A. Salmon, *Souvenirs sans fin*, vol. I, Paris, 1955, pp. 187–8, quoted in Paris and Munich 1998, p. 162.

90. Degas sent back to Manet a still life (probably Manet's *Walnuts in a Bowl*, 1866, Bührle Collection, Zurich) following a dispute. Likewise, in 1899, after a quarrel, Degas returned to Renoir a female portrait he had acquired from the artist some 20 years earlier (presumably Renoir's *Woman in Black*, 1876, The Hermitage Museum, St Petersburg). See New York 1997b, pp. 88 and 110.

91. Dumas 1996, p. 20, n. 145.

92. Freud quoted in M. Evans, 'The Englishness of Freud's Art', in Vienna and Munich 2013, p. 86.

93. Freud, quoted in Feaver 2007, p. 37.

94. Reynolds often provided certificates of authenticity on Old Master paintings for sale. See Broun 1987, p. 42.

95. B. Bryant, 'An Artist Collects: Leighton as a Collector of Painting and Drawings', in London 2010, pp. 22–4.

96. Matisse, interview with Jacques Guenne, 1925, reprinted in Flam 1995, p. 80.

97. Renoir, *Portrait of Suzanne Valadon*, about 1885, Private collection; also Courbet, *La blonde endormie*, 1857 (Fernier 226) and the painted study for the *Demoiselles des bords de Seine*, 1856 (Fernier 209). See Robert Fernier, *La vie et l'œuvre de Gustave Courbet*, catalogue raisonné, Bibliothèque des Arts, Lausanne and Paris, 1977. Vol. 1: 1819–65.

98. Matisse to Max Pellequer. See Bois 1998, p. 133, n. 250.

99. See Paris 2010, p. 178.

100. Freud, *After Cézanne*, 1999–2000, National Gallery of Australia, Canberra. Freud worked from a photograph of the Cézanne pinned to his studio walls. See Dawson 2014, p. 29.

101. Freud, *Large Interior, W11 (after Watteau)*, 1981–3, Private collection, based on J.A. Watteau's *Pierrot Content*, about 1712, Museo Thyssen-Bornemisza, Madrid.

102. Freud quoted in Jasper Sharp, 'To Sieve for Poison and Pleasure', in Vienna and Munich 2013, p. 19.

103. See Canberra 2001, p.4

Bibliography

ALBINSON, FUNNELL AND PELTZ 2010–11
C. Albinson, P. Funnell and L. Peltz, *Thomas Lawrence: Regency, Power & Brilliance*, National Portrait Gallery, London 2010–11

BAKER 1987
J. Baker, *Henry Lee McFee and Formalist Realism in American Still Life, 1923–1936*, London and Toronto 1987

BAYES 1907
W. Bayes, *The Landscapes of George Frederick Watts*, London 1907

BOIS 1993
Y.-A. Bois, *Painting as Model*, Cambridge, MA, and London 1993

BOIS 1998
Y.-A. Bois, *Matisse and Picasso*, Paris 1998, published in conjunction with an exhibition at Kimbell Art Museum, Fort Worth, TX 31 January–2 May 1999

BRAHAM AND BRUCE-GARDNER 1988
H. Braham and R. Bruce-Gardner, 'Rubens's Landscape by Moonlight', *The Burlington Magazine*, vol. 130, no. 1025 (August 1988)

BROUN 1987
F. Broun, *Sir Joshua Reynolds' Collection of Paintings*, PhD dissertation, Princeton University 1987

BRYANT 2008
B. Bryant, *G.F. Watts, Victorian Visionary*, London 2008

CANBERRA 2001
Lucian Freud, After Cézanne, National Gallery of Australia, Canberra 2001

COLUMBUS 1955
Sir Thomas Lawrence as Painter and Collector, exh. cat., Columbus Gallery of Fine Arts, Columbus, OH 7 October–13 November 1955

COMPTON 2011
M. Bills, *Painting the Nation: G. F. Watts at the Tate*, exh. cat., Watts Gallery, Compton 18 June 2011–1 January 2012

COURTHION N.D.
P. Courthion, 'Conversations avec H. Matisse', typescript, Getty Center for the History of Art and the Humanities, Archives of the History of Art, Santa Monica, CA

DAWSON 2014
D. Dawson, *A Painter's Progress: A Portrait of Lucian Freud*, London 2014

DUMAS 1996
A. Dumas, *Degas as a Collector*, Apollo Magazine Ltd / National Gallery Publications, London 1996

EMMERICH 1958
A. Emmerich, 'The Artist as Collector', Trends in Collecting, in *Art in America*, vol. 46 (Summer 1958)

ESCHOLIER 1956
R. Escholier, *Matisse ce vivant*, Paris 1956

FEAVER 2002
W. Feaver, *Lucian Freud*, exh. cat., Tate, London 2002

FEAVER 2007
W. Feaver, *Lucian Freud*, New York 2007

FINALDI, HARDING AND WALLIS 1995
G. Finaldi, E. Harding J. and Wallis, 'The Conservation of the Carracci Cartoons in the National Gallery', *NG Technical Bulletin*, vol. 16 (1995)

FLAM 1995
J. Flam, *Matisse on Art*, Berkeley, CA 1995

FREUD 2007
Freud at Work, photographs by Bruce Bernard and David Dawson; Lucian Freud in conversation with Sebastian Smee, London 2007

FREUD 2010
L. Freud, 'Some Thoughts on Painting', *Encounter*, vol. III, no. I (July 1954), Centre Pompidou, Paris 2010

GARLICK 1989
K. Garlick, *Sir Thomas Lawrence: A Complete Catalogue of the Oil Paintings*, Oxford 1989

GOULD 2004
V. Franklin Gould, *G.F. Watts, The Last Great Victorian*, London 2004

HALLETT 2014
M. Hallett, *Reynolds: Portraiture in Action*, London 2014

HERRMANN 1999
F. Herrmann, *The English as Collectors: a Documentary Sourcebook*, London 1999

JOANNIDES 2007
P. Joannides, 'The Dispersal and Formation of Sir Thomas Lawrence's Collection of Drawings by Michelangelo', in *The Drawings of Michelangelo and his Followers in the Ashmolean Museum*, Cambridge 2007

LAPAUZE 1918
H. Lapauze, 'Ingres chez Degas', in *Renaissance de l'art français et des industries de luxe*, vol. 1, no. 1 (March 1918)

LEVEY 2005
M. Levey, *Sir Thomas Lawrence*, London 2005

LONDON 1974
J. Gage, *G.F. Watts, A Nineteenth-Century Phenomenon*, exh. cat., Whitechapel Art Gallery, London 1974

LONDON 1978
T. Clifford, A. Griffiths and M. Royalton-Kisch, *Gainsborough and Reynolds in the British Museum: The Drawings of Gainsborough and Reynolds with a Survey of Mezzotints after Their Paintings, and a Study of Reynolds' Collection of Old Master Drawings*, exh. cat., British Museum, London 1978

LONDON 1987
The Artist's Eye: Lucian Freud. An Exhibition of National Gallery Paintings Selected by the Artist, exh. cat., National Gallery, London 17 June–16 August 1987

LONDON 1996
Frederic, Lord Leighton: Eminent Victorian Artist, exh. cat., Royal Academy of Arts, London 15 February–21 April 1996

LONDON 2000
Encounters: New Art from Old, exh. cat., National Gallery, London 14 June–17 September 2000

LONDON 2004
B. Bryant, *G.F. Watts: Portraits, Fame and Beauty in Victorian Society*, exh. cat., National Portrait Gallery, London 14 October 2004–9 January 2005

LONDON 2009
K. Hearn (ed.), *Van Dyck & Britain*, exh. cat., Tate, London 18 February–17 May 2009

LONDON 2010
Closer to Home: The Restoration of Leighton House and Catalogue of the Reopening Displays, Leighton House Museum, London 2010

LONDON 2012
S. Howgate with M. Auping and J. Richardson, *Lucian Freud Portraits*, exh. cat., National Portrait Gallery, London 2012

LONDON 2015a
L. Davis and M. Hallett, *Joshua Reynolds: Experiments in Paint*, exh. cat., Wallace Collection, London 12 March–7 June 2015

LONDON 2015b
L. Yee, *Magnificent Obsessions: The Artist as Collector*, exh. cat., Barbican Art Gallery, London 12 February–25 May 2015

LONDON AND COMPTON 2006
A. Staley and H. Underwood, *Painting the Cosmos: Landscapes by G.F. Watts*, exh. cat., Nevill Keating Gallery, London; Watts Gallery, Compton 2006

LONDON, PARIS AND NEW YORK 2002–3
Matisse-Picasso, exh. cat., Tate, London; Grand Palais, Paris; MoMA, New York 2002–3

MANNINGS AND POSTLE 2000
D. Mannings and M. Postle, *Sir Joshua Reynolds: A Complete Catalogue of His Paintings*, New Haven and London, 2000

MARTIGNY 2015
C. Debray, *Matisse en son temps*, exh. cat., Centre Georges Pompidou, Paris; Fondation Pierre Gianadda, Martigny 20 June–22 November 2015

MATISSE 1972
H. Matisse, *Ecrits et Propos sur l'Art*, Paris 1972

MATISSE, COUTURIER AND RAYSSIGUIER 1993
H. Matisse, M.-A. Couturier and L.-B. Rayssiguier, *La Chapelle de Vence: Journal d'une création*, Paris 1993

MONOD-FONTAINE 1984
I. Monod-Fontaine, *The Sculpture of Henri Matisse*, London 1984

MULLER 1989
J.M. Muller, *Rubens: The Artist as Collector*, Princeton 1989

NEW YORK 1997a
A. Dumas, C. Ives, S. Stein and G. Tinterow, *The Private Collection of Edgar Degas*, exh. cat., Metropolitan Museum, New York 1997

NEW YORK 1997b
C. Ives, S. Stein and J.A. Steiner, *The Private Collection of Edgar Degas: A Summary Catalogue*, Metropolitan Museum, New York 1997

NEW YORK 2009
S. Rewald, *The American Matisse: The Dealer, His Artists, His Collection*, exh. cat., Metropolitan Museum, New York 2009

NEW YORK, CHICAGO AND PARIS 2006–7
Cézanne to Picasso: Ambroise Vollard, Patron of the Avant-Garde, exh. cat., New York, Chicago and Paris 2006–7

ORMOND 1975
L. and R. Ormond, *Lord Leighton*, London 1975

OXFORD AND LONDON 1996
C. Whistler, 'The Taste for Carracci Drawings in Britain', in C. Robertson and C. Whistler, *Drawings by the Carracci from British Collections*, exh. cat., Ashmolean Museum, Oxford; London, 1996

PARIS 2002
Constable – Le choix de Lucian Freud, exh. cat., Grand Palais, Paris 2002

PARIS 2010
C. Debray (ed.), *Lucian Freud. L'Atelier*, exh. cat., Centre Pompidou, Paris 10 March–19 July 2010

PARIS AND BRISBANE 2008
Picasso & His Collection, exh. cat., Musée national Picasso, Paris, in association with Queensland Art Gallery, Brisbane 9 June–14 September 2008

PARIS, LONDON AND PHILADELPHIA 2014–15
Inventing Impressionism: Paul Durand-Ruel and the Modern Art Market, exh. cat., Réunion des Musées Nationaux, Paris; National Gallery, London; Philadelphia Museum of Art, Philadelphia, 2014–15

PARIS, LOS ANGELES AND PHILADELPHIA 2009–10
Renoir au XXème siècle, exh. cat., Grand Palais, Paris; LACMA, Los Angeles; Philadelphia Museum of Art, Philadelphia, 2009–10

PARIS AND MUNICH 1998
H. Seckel-Klein and E. Chevrière, *Picasso Collectionneur*, exh. cat., Réunion des Musées Nationaux, Paris; Kunsthalle, Munich 1998

PHILADELPHIA 2009
Cézanne and Beyond, exh. cat., Philadelphia Museum of Art, PA 2009

PLYMOUTH 2009
S. Smiles (ed.), *Sir Joshua Reynolds: The Acquisition of Genius*, exh. cat., Plymouth City Museum and Art Gallery 21 November 2009–20 February 2010

REWALD 1996
J. Rewald, *The Paintings of Paul Cézanne: A Catalogue Raisonné*, New York 1996

REYNOLDS 1945
'Sir Joshua Reynolds' Collection of Pictures, I', *The Burlington Magazine*, no. 507 (June 1945); no. 510 (September 1945); no. 512 (November 1945)

RICHARDSON 1991, 1996, 2007
J. Richardson, *A Life of Picasso, 1907–1917*, vols I, II & III, London 1991, 1996, 2007

SICKERT 1917
W. Sickert, 'Degas', *The Burlington Museum for Connoisseurs*, vol. 31, no. 176 (November 1917)

SMEE 2005
S. Smee, *Lucian Freud 1996–2005*, London 2005

SPURLING 1998
H. Spurling, *The Unknown Matisse: Man of the North 1869–1908*, vol. 1, London 1998

SPURLING 2005
H. Spurling, *Matisse The Master*, vol. 2, London 2005

STOURTON AND SEBAG-MONTEFIORE 2012
J. Stourton and C. Sebag-Montefiore, *The British as Art Collectors: from the Tudors to the Present*, London 2012

TWIST 2006
A. Twist, *A Life of John Julius Angerstein, 1735–1823: Widening Circles in Finance, Philanthropy and the Arts in Eighteenth Century London*, Lewiston, New York 2006.

VIENNA AND MUNICH 2013
S. Haag and J. Sharp (eds), *Lucian Freud*, exh. cat., Kunsthistorisches Museum, Vienna; Munich 2013

VOLLARD 1936
A. Vollard, *Recollections of a Picture Dealer*, London 1936

WARK 1959
R.R. Wark (ed.), *Joshua Reynolds: Discourses on Art*, San Marino 1959

WILLIAMS 1831
D.E. Williams, *The Life and Correspondence of Sir Thomas Lawrence, Kt …*, vol. II, London 1831

WOOD 1990
J. Wood, 'Van Dyck's "Cabinet de Titien": The Contents and Dispersal of His Collection', *The Burlington Magazine*, vol. 132, no. 1051 (October 1990)

List of Lenders

ABERDEEN
Aberdeen Art Gallery & Museums

CAMBRIDGE
The Syndics of the Fitzwilliam Museum, University of Cambridge

COPENHAGEN
Ordrupgaard

EDINBURGH
Scottish National Gallery

GUILDFORD
Watts Gallery

LEEDS
Leeds Museums and Galleries

LONDON
The British Museum
Royal Academy of Arts
Tate

NEW YORK
The Elkon Gallery

OXFORD
The Ashmolean Museum

PARIS
Centre Pompidou, Paris. Musée national d'art moderne/Centre de création industrielle
Musée d'Orsay
Petit Palais, Musée des Beaux-Arts de la Ville de Paris

PHILADELPHIA
Philadelphia Museum of Art

YORK
Castle Howard Collection

The Royal Collection/ HM Queen Elizabeth II
Collection of Ömer Koç
Collection Jasper Johns
The Tia Collection

And those private collectors who wish to remain anonymous

List of Exhibited Works

Freud

Lucian Freud
Self Portrait: Reflection
2002
Oil on canvas
66 × 50.8 cm
Private collection CAT. 1

Paul Cézanne
*Afternoon in Naples
(L'après-midi à Naples)*
1876–7
Oil on canvas
29.5 × 39.5 cm
Private collection CAT. 3

Lucian Freud
After Breakfast
2001
Oil on canvas
41 × 58.4 cm
Private collection CAT. 4

Frank Auerbach
Birthday card to Lucian Freud, drawn
from a photograph by Kevin Davies
of Auerbach and Freud at the Cock
Tavern, Smithfield
2002
Lent by the Syndics of the Fitzwilliam
Museum, University of Cambridge FIG. 2

Jean-Baptiste-Camille Corot
Italian Woman, or *Woman with
Yellow Sleeve (L'Italienne)*
about 1870
Oil on canvas
73 × 59 cm
The National Gallery, London.
Accepted in lieu of Inheritance Tax by
HM Government from the estate of
Lucian Freud and allocated to the
National Gallery, 2012
(NG662) CAT. 2

Hilaire-Germain-Edgar Degas
*Portrait of a Woman:
Head resting on One Hand*
Cast after 1918
Bronze
12.3 × 17.5 × 16.2 cm
Leeds Museums and Galleries
(Leeds Art Gallery) FIG. 5

John Constable
Portrait of Laura Moubray
1808
Oil on canvas
44.5 × 35.5 cm
Scottish National Gallery, Edinburgh.
Accepted by HM Government in lieu of
Inheritance Tax from the estate of Lucian
Freud and allocated to the Scottish
National Gallery, 2013 CAT. 5

Lucian Freud
Portrait Head
2001
Etching
75 × 60 cm
Private collection
Not illustrated

Matisse

Henri Matisse
Self Portrait
1918
Oil on canvas
65 × 54 cm
Paris, musée d'Orsay, dépôt au
musée départemental Henri Matisse,
Le Cateau-Cambrésis, donation de
Mme Jean Matisse, 1979 CAT. 6

Paul Cézanne
Three Bathers
1879–82
Oil on canvas
55 × 52 cm
Petit Palais, Musée des Beaux-Arts
de la Ville de Paris CAT. 7

Henri Matisse
Back III (Nu de dos, troisième état)
1916–17
Bronze
185 × 111.5 × 22.5 cm
Centre Pompidou, Paris. Musée national
d'art moderne/Centre de création
industrielle. Dation Pierre Matisse, 1991.
En dépôt depuis 1993: Musée d'art
moderne de la Ville de Paris (Paris)
Not illustrated

Paul Gauguin
Young Man with a Flower behind his Ear
1891
Oil on canvas
45.4 × 33.5 cm
Property from a distinguished private
collection – courtesy of Christie's CAT. 8

Henri Matisse
Portrait of Greta Moll
1908
Oil on canvas
93 × 73.5 cm
The National Gallery, London. Bought, 1979
(NG6450) CAT. 10

Hilaire-Germain-Edgar Degas
Combing the Hair ('La Coiffure')
about 1896
Oil on canvas
114.3 × 146.7 cm
The National Gallery, London.
Bought (Knapping Fund), 1937
(NG4865) CAT. 12

Henri Matisse
*The Inattentive Reader
(La liseuse distraite)*
1919
Oil on canvas
73 × 92.4 cm
Tate: Bequeathed by Montague
Shearman through the Contemporary
Art Society 1940 CAT. 13

Paul Signac
*The Green House, Venice
(La maison verte, Venise)*
1905
Oil on canvas
46 × 55.2 cm
Private collection CAT. 9

Paul Cézanne
Madame Cézanne
1886–7
Oil on canvas
46.8 × 38.9 cm
Philadelphia Museum of Art:
The Samuel S. White 3rd and
Vera White Collection, 1967 CAT. 11

Pablo Picasso
Portrait of a Woman: Dora Maar
20 January 1942
Gouache on paper
40.5 × 30.3 cm
Private collection, United Kingdom CAT. 14

Pablo Picasso
Portrait of Dora Maar
1942
Oil on canvas
61.6 × 50.5 cm
Courtesy The Elkon Gallery,
New York City CAT. 15

Degas: I – Contemporaries

Hilaire-Germain-Edgar Degas
Self Portrait
1857–8
Oil on paper
47 × 32 cm
The Tia Collection FIG. 1

Paul Gauguin
A Vase of Flowers
1896
Oil on canvas
64 × 74 cm
The National Gallery, London. Bought, 1918
(NG3289) CAT. 32

Camille Pissarro
Landscape at Pontoise
1872
Oil on canvas
46 × 55 cm
The Ashmolean Museum, Oxford.
Bequeathed by Montague Shearman
through the Contemporary Art Society,
1940 CAT. 26

Alfred Sisley
The Flood. Banks of the Seine, Bougival
1873
Oil on canvas
50 × 65.5 cm
Ordrupgaard, Copenhagen CAT. 27

Paul Cézanne
Bather with Outstretched Arm (study)
1883–5
Oil on canvas
33 × 24 cm
Collection Jasper Johns CAT. 33

Jacques-Emile Blanche
Francis Poictevin
1887
Oil on canvas
26.7 × 16.5 cm
Tate: Presented by Miss Hilda Trevelyan
1939
(L689) CAT. 31

Edouard Manet
Woman with a Cat
about 1880–2
Oil on canvas
92.1 × 73 cm
Tate: Purchased 1918
(L675) CAT. 28

Edouard Manet
The Execution of Maximilian
about 1867–8
Oil on canvas, four fragments mounted
193 × 284 cm
The National Gallery, London. Bought, 1918
(NG3294) CAT. 30

Georges Jeanniot
Conscripts (Conscrits)
1894
Oil on canvas
72.7 × 86.3 cm
Collection of Ömer Koç CAT. 29

Hilaire-Germain-Edgar Degas
Young Spartans Exercising
about 1860
Oil on canvas
109.5 × 155 cm
The National Gallery, London.
Bought, Courtauld Fund, 1924
(NG3860) Not illustrated

Jean-Louis Forain
The Tribunal (Le tribunal)
about 1902–3
Oil on canvas
60.3 × 73 cm
Tate: Purchased 1918
Not illustrated

Degas: II – The Masters

Hilaire-Germain-Edgar Degas
Self Portrait
1855
Oil on paper laid on canvas
81.3 × 64.5 cm
Paris, musée d'Orsay CAT. 16

Jean-Auguste-Dominique Ingres
Angelica saved by Ruggiero
1819–39
Oil on canvas
47.6 × 39.4 cm
The National Gallery, London. Bought, 1918
(NG3292) CAT. 18

Jean-Auguste-Dominique Ingres
Dante offering his Works to Homer
(study for *The Apotheosis of Homer*)
about 1827 and about 1864–5
Oil on three pieces of canvas mounted
on wood
38 × 35.5 cm
Ordrupgaard, Copenhagen CAT. 19

Jean-Auguste-Dominique Ingres
Pindar and Ictinus
probably 1830–67
Oil on canvas laid down on panel
34.9 × 27.9 cm
The National Gallery, London. Bought, 1918
(NG3293) CAT. 20

Jean-Auguste-Dominique Ingres
Monsieur de Norvins
1811–12
Oil on canvas laid down on panel
97.2 × 78.7 cm
The National Gallery, London. Bought, 1918
(NG3291) CAT. 17

Jean-Auguste-Dominique Ingres
Oedipus and the Sphinx
about 1826
Oil on canvas
17.5 × 13.7 cm
The National Gallery, London. Bought, 1918
(NG3290) Not illustrated

Hilaire-Germain-Edgar Degas
Portrait of Elena Carafa
about 1875
Oil on canvas
70.1 × 55 cm
The National Gallery, London. Bought,
Courtauld Fund, 1926
(NG4167) FIG. 6

Hilaire-Germain-Edgar Degas
Study of a Sky (Etude de ciel)
about 1869
Pastel on grey-blue paper
29 × 48 cm
Paris, musée d'Orsay CAT. 24

Eugène Delacroix
Study of the Sky at Sunset
1849–50
Pastel and coloured chalk on blue paper
22.8 × 26.8 cm
The British Museum, London CAT. 23

Hilaire-Germain-Edgar Degas
Beach Scene
about 1869–70
Oil (essence) on paper on canvas
47.5 × 82.9 cm
The National Gallery, London.
Sir Hugh Lane Bequest, 1917
(NG3247) Not illustrated

Théodore Rousseau
The Valley of Saint-Vincent
1830
Oil on paper laid on canvas
18.2 × 32.4 cm
The National Gallery, London. Bought, 1918
(NG3296) Not illustrated

Hilaire-Germain-Edgar Degas
Promenade beside the Sea
about 1860
Oil on canvas
22.5 × 32.5 cm
The Gere Collection, on long-term loan
to the National Gallery
(L819) Not illustrated

Jean-Baptiste-Camille Corot
*The Roman Campagna, with the
Claudian Aqueduct*
probably 1826
Oil on paper laid on canvas
22.8 × 34 cm
The National Gallery, London. Bought at
the Degas sale (with a special grant), 1918
(NG3285) CAT. 25

Louis-Gustave Ricard
Portrait of a Man
probably 1866
Oil on canvas
64.1 × 54.6 cm
The National Gallery, London. Bought, 1918
(NG3297) Not illustrated

Probably by Pierre Andrieu
Still Life with Fruit and Flowers
probably about 1850–64
Oil on canvas
65.8 × 81 cm
The National Gallery, London. Bought, 1964
(NG6349) Not illustrated

Eugène Delacroix
Louis-Auguste Schwiter
1826–30
Oil on canvas
217.8 × 143.5 cm
The National Gallery, London. Bought, 1918
(NG3286) CAT. 21

Eugène Delacroix
Hercules rescuing Hesione
1852
Oil on canvas
24.5 × 47.5 cm
Ordrupgaard, Copenhagen CAT. 22

Eugène Delacroix
Abel Widmer
about 1824
Oil on canvas
59.7 × 48.3 cm
The National Gallery, London. Bought, 1918
(NG3287) Not illustrated

Leighton and Watts

Frederic, Lord Leighton
Self Portrait
1882
Oil on canvas
34.5 × 29.7 cm
Aberdeen Art Gallery &
Museums Collections CAT. 34

Jean-Baptiste-Camille Corot
The Four Times of Day
about 1858
Oil on wood

The Four Times of Day: Morning
142.2 × 72.3 cm
(NG6651)

The Four Times of Day: Noon
142.2 × 62.2 cm
(NG6652)

The Four Times of Day: Evening
142.2 × 72.3 cm
(NG6653)

The Four Times of Day: Night
142.2 × 64.7 cm
(NG6654)

The National Gallery, London. Bought
with the assistance of the Art Fund
(with a contribution from The Wolfson
Foundation), 2014 CAT. 36

Frederic, Lord Leighton
Trees at Cliveden
1880s
Oil on canvas
42 × 28 cm
Private collection CAT. 38

Jean-Baptiste-Camille Corot
Evening on the Lake
about 1872
Oil on canvas
25.1 × 36.2 cm
The National Gallery, London.
Salting Bequest, 1910
(NG2627) FIG. 8

Frederic, Lord Leighton
Aynhoe Park
1860s
Oil on canvas
34.3 × 40.6 cm
Lent from a private collection, courtesy of
The Ashmolean Museum, Oxford CAT. 37

Possibly by Jacopo Tintoretto
Jupiter and Semele
about 1545
Oil on spruce
22.7 × 65.4 cm
The National Gallery, London. Bought, 1896
(NG1476) CAT. 39

Eugène Delacroix
The Muse of Orpheus
1845–7
Pen and ink heightened with
oil on paper, laid on canvas
21.3 × 25.5 cm
Lent by the Syndics of the Fitzwilliam
Museum, University of Cambridge CAT. 35

George Frederic Watts
Self Portrait in a Red Robe
about 1853
Oil on canvas
154.9 × 74.9 cm
Watts Gallery CAT. 40

Probably by Girolamo Macchietti
A Knight of S. Stefano
after 1563
Oil on wood
209.5 × 121.2 cm
The National Gallery, London. Presented
by G.F. Watts RA, 1861
(NG670) CAT. 41

French (?)
Profile Portrait of a Young Man
possibly about 1580
Oil on paper mounted on canvas
38.5 × 28.5 cm
The National Gallery, London. Presented
by G.F. Watts, 1885
(NG1190) FIG. 4

George Frederic Watts
Autumn
1901–3
Oil on canvas
134.6 × 73.7 cm
Watts Gallery CAT. 42

Lawrence

Sir Thomas Lawrence
Self Portrait
about 1825
Oil on canvas
91 × 71.4 cm
Lent by the Royal Academy of Arts,
London CAT. 43

Raphael
An Allegory ('Vision of a Knight')
about 1504
Oil on poplar
17.1 × 17.3 cm
The National Gallery, London. Bought, 1847
(NG213) CAT. 44

Guido Reni
The Coronation of the Virgin
about 1607
Oil on copper
66.6 × 48.8 cm
The National Gallery, London.
Bequeathed by William Wells, 1847
(NG214) CAT. 47

Sir Thomas Lawrence
*Sir Francis Baring, First Baronet,
John Baring and Charles Wall*
1806–7
Oil on canvas
156 × 226 cm
Private collection CAT. 49

After Hugo van der Goes
The Death of the Virgin
probably after 1500
Oil on oak
38.7 × 35.6 cm
The National Gallery, London. Bought, 1860
(NG658) Not illustrated

Agostino Carracci
A Woman borne off by a Sea God (?)
about 1599
Charcoal and white chalk (a grey wash
applied later over the whole) on paper
203.2 × 410.2 cm
The National Gallery, London. Presented
by Lord Francis Egerton, 1837
(NG148) CAT. 45

Sir Anthony van Dyck
*Carlo and Ubaldo see Rinaldo
conquered by Love for Armida*
1634–5
Oil on wood
57 × 41.5 cm
The National Gallery, London. Bought, 1871
(NG877.2) CAT. 46

Sir Thomas Lawrence
John Julius Angerstein, aged over 80
1824
Oil on canvas
91.5 × 71 cm
The National Gallery, London. Presented
by William IV, 1836
(NG129) FIG. 7

Follower of Rembrandt
A Seated Man with a Stick
perhaps 1675–1725
Oil on canvas
137.5 × 104.8 cm
The National Gallery, London. Presented
by Sir George Beaumont, 1823/8
(NG51) CAT. 48

Reynolds

Sir Joshua Reynolds
Self Portrait
about 1780
Oil on panel
127 × 101.6 cm
Lent by the Royal Academy of Arts,
London CAT. 50

Nicolas Poussin
The Adoration of the Shepherds
about 1633–4
Oil on canvas
97.2 × 74 cm
The National Gallery, London. Bought
with a special grant and contribution from
The Art Fund, 1957
(NG6277) CAT. 58

Jacopo Bassano
The Good Samaritan
about 1562–3
Oil on canvas
102.1 × 79.7 cm
The National Gallery, London. Bought, 1856
(NG277) CAT. 53

Giovanni Bellini
The Agony in the Garden
about 1465
Egg on wood
81.3 × 127 cm
The National Gallery, London. Bought, 1863
(NG726) CAT. 51

Sébastien Bourdon
The Return of the Ark
1659
Oil on canvas
105.3 × 134.6 cm
The National Gallery, London. Presented
by Sir George Beaumont, 1826
(NG64) FIG. 3

Thomas Gainsborough
Girl with Pigs
1781–2
Oil on canvas
125.6 × 148.6 cm
From the Castle Howard Collection CAT. 59

Sir Anthony van Dyck
*Portrait of George Gage with
Two Attendants*
probably 1622–3
Oil on canvas
115 × 113.5 cm
The National Gallery, London. Bought, 1824
(NG49) CAT. 56

Rembrandt
The Lamentation over the Dead Christ
about 1635
Oil on paper and pieces of canvas,
mounted onto oak
31.9 × 26.7 cm
The National Gallery, London. Presented
by Sir George Beaumont, 1823/8
(NG43) CAT. 54

Rembrandt
Lamentation over the Dead Christ
about 1634–5
Pen and brown ink and brown wash,
with red and perhaps some black chalk,
reworked in oils 'en grisaille'; framing
lines in thin black oil paint; on paper
21.6 × 25.4 cm
The British Museum, London CAT. 55

Adam Elsheimer
The Baptism of Christ
about 1599
Oil on copper
28.1 × 21 cm
The National Gallery, London.
Presented by Henry Wagner, 1924
(NG3904) Not illustrated

After Michelangelo
Leda and the Swan
after 1530
Oil on canvas
105.4 × 141 cm
The National Gallery, London. Presented
by the Duke of Northumberland, 1838
(NG1868) CAT. 52

Style of Sir Anthony van Dyck
The Horses of Achilles
1635–45
Oil on canvas
105.5 × 91.5 cm
The National Gallery, London.
Bequeathed by Lord Farnborough, 1838
(NG156) CAT. 57

Van Dyck

Sir Anthony van Dyck
Self Portrait
about 1629
Oil on canvas
80 × 61 cm
Private collection CAT. 60

Titian
Portrait of Gerolamo (?) Barbarigo
about 1510
Oil on canvas
81.2 × 66.3 cm
The National Gallery, London. Bought, 1904
(NG1944) CAT. 61

Sir Anthony van Dyck
*Lord John Stuart and his Brother,
Lord Bernard Stuart*
about 1638
Oil on canvas
237.5 × 146.1 cm
The National Gallery, London. Bought, 1988
(NG6518) FIG. 9

Titian
*The Vendramin Family, venerating a Relic
of the True Cross*
1540–5
Oil on canvas
206.1 × 288.5 cm
The National Gallery, London. Bought
with a special grant and contributions
from Samuel Courtauld, Sir Joseph
Duveen, The Art Fund and the Phillips
Fund, 1929.
(NG4452) CAT. 62

Sir Anthony van Dyck
*Thomas Killigrew and William,
Lord Crofts (?)*
1638
Oil on canvas
132.9 × 144.1 cm
The Royal Collection/
HM Queen Elizabeth II CAT. 63

Acknowledgements

This exhibition and book would not have happened without the continued support of Gabriele Finaldi, Director of the National Gallery, and Nicholas Penny, former Director; I am deeply grateful for the trust they placed in the project. For their constant encouragement and inestimable help I would like to thank Caroline Campbell and Christopher Riopelle; the introductory essay to this book benefited from their insightful comments, as well as those from Susanna Avery-Quash, to whom I express my gratitude. Christopher Riopelle supported the genesis and development of this exhibition with unflinching enthusiasm and wrote entries for this book. I would also like to thank Allison Goudie, Sarah Herring and Harriet O'Neill for their contributions. This publication benefited from the attentive care of Suzanne Bosman, Rachel Giles, Jan Green, Adrian Hunt, Penny Le Tissier, Louisa Newton and Linda Schofield. I am also grateful to Susan Foister, Jane Knowles and Letizia Treves, and thank Sylvie Broussine and Lucy West for their assistance.

The exhibition owes a great debt to the Courtauld Institute's 'Curating the Art Museum' MA; students Martha Ellis-Leach and Kirsten Tambling provided invaluable help at various stages of its making. I would like to express my gratitude to Giovanna Bertazzoni, David Dawson, Michael Findlay and Wanda de Guébriant for their energetic assistance and for generously sharing their knowledge and expertise. I am thankful to the staff at the Archives Matisse at Issy-les-Moulineaux, the Pierre Matisse Gallery Archives at the Morgan Library, and the Service de la Documentation at the Musée d'Orsay, who facilitated my visits and research. The section of this exhibition devoted to Degas as a collector is entirely indebted to Ann Dumas's unrivalled scholarship, showcased in outstanding exhibitions at the National Gallery and the Metropolitan Museum of Art in 1996 and 1997.

I am thankful to the National Gallery Collection Curators who supported this exhibition, and to museums as well as private collectors who contributed loans. Works have been entrusted to us thanks to the help of Christie's. I would like to extend my sincere thanks to all those who assisted this project in a variety of ways: Paul Ackroyd, Rhian Addison, Gabriel Badea-Päun, Sophie Ballinger, Claire Bernardi, Francis Broun, Barbara Bryant, Stephanie Carlton, David Chan, Hugo Chapman, Isabelle Collet, Caroline Collier, Caroline Corbeau-Parsons, François Croquette, Cécile Debray, Patrice Deparpe, Elise Dubreuil, Anne-Birgitte Fonsmark, Howard Freeman, Isabelle Gaëtan, Véronique Gérard-Powell, Charlotte Gere, Mari Griffith, Antony Griffiths, Colin Harrison, Gill Hart, Nick Howard, Nancy Ireson, Larry Keith, Jo Kent, Louisa Krzyz, Alice Lamarre-Bourgoin, Christophe Leribault, Hannah Litvack, Anne Montfort, Alexandra Moskalenko, Philip Mould, Jacqueline Munck, Jane Munro, Patrick Noon, Chris Oberon, Pilar Ordovas, Richard Ormond, Patrick O'Sullivan, Edouard Papet, Sylvie Patry, Belinda Phillpot, Caroline Porter, Xavier Rey, Christopher Ridgway, Joseph Rishel, Rosario Saxe-Coburg, Thomas Seydoux, Desmond Shawe-Taylor, Mark Slattery, Alison Smith, Frances Spalding, Jennifer Thompson, Nicholas Tromans, Colin Wiggins, Humphrey Wine and Lydia Yee.

My thanks also go to Rickie Burman, Ursula Faure-Romanelli, Judith Kerr, Susie Murphy and Amy Spolton of the Development Department of the National Gallery for their energetic support of this project. Merci à Luc, Edgar et Gabriel pour leur patience, et à Jean-Pierre et Marie-Odile Josse. The publication of this book is generously supported by Frank and Sylviane Destribats to whom I express my profound gratitude.

Photographic Credits

Published to accompany the exhibition
Painters' Paintings: From Freud to Van Dyck
The National Gallery, London
23 June – 4 September 2016

This catalogue has been generously supported by

The exhibition has been supported by

The Thompson Family Charitable Trust

BLAVATNIK FAMILY FOUNDATION

Athene Foundation
Mr Colin Clark
Philippe and Stephanie Camu
and several other donors

This exhibition has been made possible by the provision of insurance through
the Government Indemnity Scheme. The National Gallery would like to thank
HM Government for providing Government Indemnity and the Department for
Culture, Media and Sport and Arts Council England for arranging the indemnity.

This edition published in Great Britain in 2016 by
National Gallery Company Limited
St Vincent House
30 Orange Street
London WC2H 7HH
www.nationalgallery.co.uk

ISBN 9781857096118
1042145

British Library Cataloguing-in-Publication Data. A catalogue record is available
from the British Library.

Publisher Jan Green
Project Editor Rachel Giles
Editor Linda Schofield
Picture Researcher Suzanne Bosman
Production Jane Hyne and Penny Le Tissier
Designed by Adrian Hunt
Origination by DL Imaging, London
Printed in Italy by Conti TipoColor

All measurements give height before width

Front cover: **Lucian Freud**, *Self Portrait: Reflection*, 2002; detail of cat. 1

Back cover: **Jean-Baptiste-Camille Corot**, *Italian Woman*, or *Woman with Yellow Sleeve (L'Italienne)*, about 1870; detail of cat. 2

Pages 2–3: **Paul Gauguin**, *A Vase of Flowers*, 1896; detail of cat. 32